21 Steps to Reprogram Your Mind

By

Dr. Sahila

About the author 4
Introduction 6
21 Steps to Reprogram Your Mind. 6
Depression, Anxiety & Self-Pity 8
STEP 1: Lack of meaning in life- 8
STEP 2: Inferiority complex 11
STEP 3: Resolve the conscious problems first. 14
STEP 4: Discover and eradicate subconscious problems. 18
Negativity, Fear & Guilt 22
STEP 5: Stop feeling guilty about the past. 22
STEP 6: Small dissatisfaction is necessary to drive you higher. 25
STEP 7: Stop comparing yourself to others. 28
STEP 8: Do the work that suits your personality. 34
Anger, Hatred and Foul mouth 38
STEP 9: When we do not forgive others, it changes overtime to hatred. 38
Step 10-Avoid these 4 things while conversing with people. ... 41
STEP 11-Learn to first relax yourself. 45
The Human MIND 51
STEP 12- 5 states of mind 51
STEP 13: Live totally in the now 55
Ignorance is the bedrock of all suffering 70
Step 14- Ignorant person is far more dangerous than an innocent person. 70

Step 15- Remove the obstacles in your path or kleshas. 74

Step 16- Every illness originates from the mind. 79

What is Suffering or Dukha? 85

Step 17-Suffering is the state of undergoing constant pain or distress. 85

Step 18- Negative mind can never give you a positive life. 91

Step 19- Types of suffering.. 96

Steps to overcome suffering 100

Step 20- Treat the cause not the symptoms........................... 100

Step 21- Power of Autosuggestion, Humor & Pranayama...... 111

Bonus Chapter: Addictions.. 118

About the author

Dr. Sahila, M.D; M.B.B.S (Sahila is her pen name) is a US trained Internal Medicine doctor. Sahila began her career as most bright young doctors do; by treating illnesses with the latest in modern medicine. But her personal experience of watching her parents suffer from painful diseases and death led her to question the modern approach to good health. While most doctors are focused on treating conditions, Dr. Sahila wondered, why isn't there more focus on preventing illnesses? This thought process led her on a beautiful path of discovery. At the peak of her career, she quit the traditional way of practicing medicine and has since been practicing and promoting a more wholesome way to prevent illnesses. She is 44 years old and a mother of three children who makes aging look beautiful and desirable.

Dr. Sahila has been trained in yoga by renowned gurus like Akshar Yoga (India) and face yoga by experts like Manasi Gulati. She has learned Pranayama techniques from Sadhguru. She has taken courses in Ayurveda from Dr. Bhaswati Bhattacharya and Dr. Vasant Lad and several other renowned Ayurveda practitioners. Extensive hours spent studying and researching Yoga taught by ancient Yogis like Patanjali and Swami Satyananda Saraswati and Swami Vivekananda have opened her eyes and mind to ancient wisdom.

Dr. Sahila has produced more than 100 videos online, close to 45 podcasts and teaches her methods to achieve wellness to hundreds of students online. She conducts free weekly meditation classes on FB for thousands of followers free of cost. She uses her own methods to teach 'Wholesome Yoga and Wholesome Meditation' on par with international standards. Her students have the unique opportunity to learn yoga and meditation from a renowned Internal medicine doctor. She has also helped hundreds of students worldwide attain better physical and mental health standards through her life coach programs and private counseling.

Dr. Sahila is also a philanthropist who believes in giving back what she earns to underprivileged children through her projects in India. Her husband graduated from IIT, Chennai and holds a double master's degree from reputed schools in the US and is currently an MD in a reputed bank in New York. More importantly he is a huge supporter of her pursuits and goals. They have been married for 20 years and are an epitome of companionship to the younger couples. Together, they have raised close to US $150,000 to fund projects such as 'Feed the Hungry Kid' and to 'Orphan Kids Crisis Due to Covid' in India. They are also funding education for several underprivileged kids within their communities as a way of giving back to the society that raised them.

Website: www.WellnessWithSahila.com

Email: sahila@WellnessWithSahila.com.com

Other books by Dr. Sahila

- **The Chakra Handbook**
- **The Why Behind Cancer**

Introduction

21 Steps to Reprogram Your Mind.

This book is designed for people to understand their inner self. What is this inner self and how do we explore this with complete understanding? You will find answers to all of this here. The aim of this book is to assist individuals who may be going through difficult times and often feel lost or helpless. It can be used as a self-help guide or as a tool to support someone else who is currently experiencing hardship. Truly speaking all of us want only 1 thing in life- which is happiness. Indeed, the innate human desire is to experience happiness and fulfillment. And yet paradoxically, more often than not, our attempts to attain happiness lead us deeper into misery and turmoil instead.

Why does this occur? The fundamental reason lies in our misguided understanding of what true happiness is and where it originates from. Most associate it with fleeting pleasures, success, wealth or relationships. But these external factors are transient in nature and cannot guarantee lasting joy.

True happiness is an internal state of peace, contentment and meaning that arises from within – from cultivating virtues of compassion, gratitude, mindfulness and living in harmony with life's ups and downs. When our well-being depends on impermanent factors, we set ourselves up for turmoil and suffering. The descent from happiness into suffering is indeed often gradual and deceptive. As individuals strive for fleeting pleasures, they lose touch with their inner spiritual compass, neglecting daily activities that cultivate well-being and self-discipline.

Slowly but assuredly, negative patterns take predominance - comparing themselves to others, attachment to impermanent achievements, resentment over life's difficulties. Before they realize it, toxins have clouded the mind and stolen peace. Suffering then manifests itself in unexpected forms – like stress, anxiety, insomnia or relational conflicts. Yet in the thick of it, most fail to recognize suffering seeds were sown long ago by one's own search for happiness. Blinded by pain, they thrash helplessly, perpetuating the vicious cycle through addictions, bitterness or reckless actions only diving deeper into suffering state.

This is why my role as guide & wellness coach is so crucial - to enlighten souls about happiness ephemeral nature, the refuge within and daily spiritual practices or sadhana that strengthen against life's storms. With support, understanding and role models, even those deeply immersed in pain can taste freedom from it and return to their natural state of inner peace.

Pulling such souls from this suffocating panic to a place of stillness, clarity and peace is indeed a gradual process requiring empathy, wisdom and perseverance on both sides. While restoring wellness demands considerable investment of time and energy, small steps each day add up. What is most rewarding for me as a life coach is to witness the transformation - from a place of such darkness and helplessness, to one of independence, resilience and compassion for others in similar turmoil. My role in nurturing hope, empowering positive change and brightening lives is a blessing indeed.

Chapter 1

Depression, Anxiety & Self-Pity

STEP 1: Lack of meaning in life-

Lack of meaning in life is indeed a significant challenge that can lead people into depression, and in extreme cases, even suicide. It's crucial to recognize that this is not an overnight occurrence. For example, when someone fails an exam, it may trigger thoughts of being unintelligent and unworthy, which can contribute to a downward spiral. We are taught that intelligence and worthiness are determined solely by exam scores in today's society. Many highly intelligent individuals struggle with **coping mechanisms** and may not have been taught how to navigate failure or setbacks in schools and colleges.

It's concerning to see that the United States is one of the leading producers of depressed individuals globally, second only to Ukraine. The statistics show that approximately 29% of people in the US have experienced depression at least once in their lifetime. This means that there is a high likelihood that when you are in a gathering like a mall, one out of every three individuals in that gathering may be struggling with depression.

This also means that those individuals have likely been grappling with self-doubt for a considerable period, and they may just need a trigger to push them towards thoughts of self-harm. It could be a single failure in an exam, a divorce, a job loss, or the death of a loved one. When expectations and reality are significantly misaligned, a deep-rooted conflict can arise within us. We start telling ourselves repeatedly that we are not good enough, leading to a diminishing sense of self-worth.

To address these challenges, in my Yoga sessions I teach the 4A method- this method can be invaluable screening tool even before you visit your psychologist. Not to mention that today it takes minimum 1 month to get an appointment with the psychiatrist or psychologist of your choice. Steps to 4A's: **Awareness, Assess Option, Acceptance and Action**.

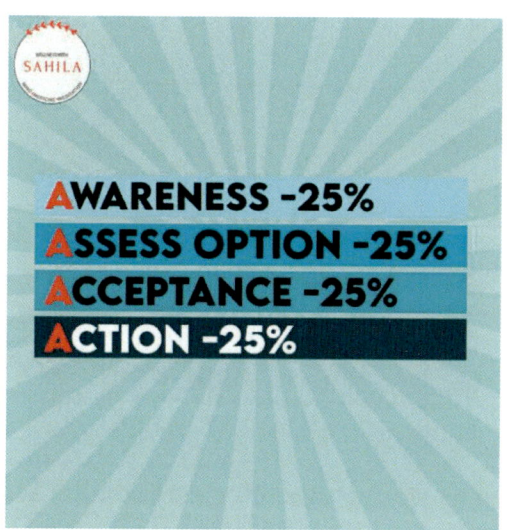

Awareness – Swadhyaya (self-study, we will be addressing swadhyaya in much more detail in later chapters in the book). This emphasizes the importance of studying ourselves, understanding our likes, dislikes, strengths, and weaknesses. In our busy lives, we often overlook self-reflection and fail to recognize our true abilities. Instead, we tend to follow the crowd, pursuing careers or activities that may not align with our strengths. However, yoga encourages us to focus on our strengths and not dwell on our weaknesses. For example, if swimming is not your forte, there's no need to keep telling yourself that you're not good at it just because your friends excel in it.

Assess options - Instead of fixating on your weaknesses, consider what actions you can take to improve your swimming skills. Taking a class or joining a program that teaches swimming might be a viable option. However, if you have tried various methods and still struggle to make progress, it's essential to reassess and explore alternative options.

Acceptance - Learning to accept that swimming may not be for you is a crucial step. Despite investing time and effort, it's important to acknowledge that swimming might not be the sport best suited for you. By accepting this reality, you free yourself from self-imposed expectations and allow yourself to move forward.

Action - Once you have accepted that swimming is not your ideal sport, it's time to take action and explore other activities that align better with your strengths and interests. By studying yourself, assessing options, and accepting your limitations, you can now venture into sports like badminton or tennis, where you can thrive and enjoy the process of growth.

Now let's apply the 4A method for a **troubled marriage** or a couple facing issues in their marriage contemplating a divorce. Spend an equal amount of time and effort in each of these 4 areas and start practicing in the same hierarchy moving from awareness to action.

Awareness- Self-study - Before jumping to conclusions about a troubled marriage, it's crucial to engage in self-reflection. Bring awareness to your marriage and ask yourself what is wrong, what is missing, and what is making you unhappy. Take the time to understand your own feelings and perspectives.

Assess options - Once you have identified the issues in your marriage, it's important to explore potential solutions. Consider what actions you can take to improve the situation and what expectations you have from your spouse. Seeking counseling or openly communicating with your partner about your concerns can be valuable steps to take.

Acceptance - In this step, it's essential to come to terms with the reality of your spouse's current capabilities. For example, if your spouse's busy career prevents them from being home often, accepting that they are willing to spend weekends with you can be a positive resolution. Acknowledge what is within their capacity at the moment.

Action - After going through the previous steps consciously and putting effort into understanding, assessing, and accepting, it's time to act. Implement the changes or compromises that both you and your spouse have agreed upon and see where they lead. With consistent effort and open communication, many couples can find solutions to their problems without resorting to depression or thoughts of ending the relationship.

STEP 2: Inferiority complex

The key difference between individuals who feel normal and those who believe they lack talent lies in their perception of themselves. Many people mistakenly assume that only famous celebrities or others are truly talented, while they consider themselves to be average or ordinary. However, what they fail to realize is that talent is often developed through recognizing and harnessing one's potential. Each one of us possesses unique gifts and abilities. The difference lies in the fact that those who are recognized as talented have embraced and tapped into their own potential. This realization sets them apart and allows them to shine.

On the other hand, those who believe they are not special or gifted often develop what is known as an inferiority complex.

What are signs of inferiority complex?

They feel physically and mentally inferior to the people around them.
They withdraw themselves from social activities.
They constantly feel insecure or unworthy.
They find themselves always comparing themselves to others.
They have an inability to complete tasks.
They have constant anxiety or insomnia.

Type 1 inferiority complex - Individuals with this type of inferiority complex feel that they lack knowledge compared to others. However, instead of taking action to acquire more knowledge and improve themselves, they tend to wallow in self-pity. This mindset can be detrimental as it prevents personal growth and keeps them stuck in a cycle of feeling inadequate.

Type 2 inferiority complex - Individuals with this type of inferiority complex also believe that they lack knowledge compared to others. However, instead of addressing their insecurities in a healthy manner, they resort to putting others down to make themselves feel superior. This behavior is toxic and not conducive to personal development or positive relationships with others.

Both types of inferiority complex are detrimental to personal growth and well-being. Rather than succumbing to self-pity or resorting to negative behavior, our primary goal should always be to acquire more knowledge and improve ourselves in the fields that interest us.

Ways to acquire knowledge

Books- Always make it a point to read minimum one book a week. In whatever field you wish to excel, or you are interested in. I read at least 2 books per week. Many great people have recommended that reading books is a good way of acquiring new wisdom time and again.

Podcasts- for people who don't like reading listening to podcasts is the new thing. Pick your favorite author or speaker or writer and listen to what knowledge they must share. Please don't use social media for knowledge acquiring. One can use social media as a medium to get introduced to new people.

Concept explanation- try to explain a new concept that you learnt or acquired to your friends or group of people. This will build confidence and also allow you to listen to what you're saying. Speaking out loud is different from speaking to yourself. Your modulations will change, your tone will change based on people's expressions and body language. This will enhance your learning capacity and prepare you for bigger stage or groups of people. Most importantly you will start believing in yourself and confidence will build.

Microlearning- learning about a well-defined new skillset or chunked content that is easy to absorb and learn. For example, you want to learn a new computer language and you find a skilled person who specializes only in that specific language and this way your time and effort is completely focused on learning that specific skillset. Similarly, chakra healing program is a defined skill set that I teach in 10 packed sessions for HUA (Hindu University of America) and during this time you are focused on learning and applying this method with the intention to heal. (for more information on this read my book- Chakra Handbook published in 2021)

STEP 3: Resolve the conscious problems first.

When we start asking ourselves deep and introspective questions, we can begin to uncover the hidden layers of our conscious problems. It is important to identify and address visible **problems** like anger, fear, jealousy, hatred, self-pity, and lack of confidence. These are like veils that overshadow our true inner selves. In the practice of Yoga, we believe that everyone possesses both good and bad qualities. By removing the negative aspects and addressing our inner demons, we allow the goodness within us to shine forth. Hence the goal of yoga is not perfection, but rather the pursuit of excellence.

It is crucial to recognize that the visible problems we observe are just the tip of the iceberg. The majority, the significant 70 percent, remains hidden beneath the surface. Similar to an iceberg, closer examination and self-reflection are required to uncover the deeper layers of our subconscious struggles.

Examples of self-reflecting questions to identify conscious problems–

Why am I getting angry with my son?
Why do I hate seeing my boss?
Why am I not happy in this relationship?
Why am I not sleeping well at night?

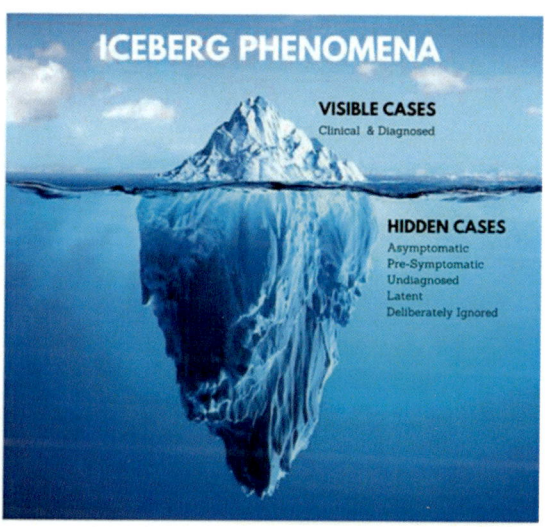

All these questions and visible problems are like warning signs, indicating that something is amiss in your life. It is crucial to pay attention to them and bring your senses and mind into focus. Conscious problems act as a wake-up call to the deeper subconscious problems that may be affecting your well-being. Unfortunately, only a small percentage, around 10 percent, heed this wake-up call. The majority, the remaining 90 percent, choose to ignore the warning signs and continue to suffer silently.

For those who ignore the warning signs, their anger increases, frustration persists, sadness grows, sleeplessness gets worse. Eventually they culminate into complex illnesses requiring medical attention like High BP, Insomnia, Anxiety, Depression etc. When you wholeheartedly practice yoga and meditation, it has the power to bring forth the questions that you have been avoiding. It can initiate a transformative shift in your life. Allow me to share my personal experience as an example. (Most of my readers from previous books have said that sharing real life experiences makes their understanding of the topic more worthy).

Ten years ago in 2013, when my father passed away, I spiraled into a state of Bipolar Depression (alternating moods of high & low). However, that depression was merely the tip of the iceberg for me. It was the culmination of all the things I had been ignoring and neglecting in my life. One of the key areas was my relationship with my three children. Deep down, I knew I was not spending enough quality time with them, and it deeply saddened me. Yet, I kept convincing myself that things would magically get better, that my work would change one day. However, the reality was that my work only became busier, with weekend shifts, night calls, and an ever-growing workload. One can only imagine the stress of a doctor's life coupled with the duties of a mother of 3 kids.

It took the wake-up call to my father's passing and my subsequent depression to realize the importance of addressing these issues. It was a pivotal moment that propelled me to reassess my priorities and make significant changes in my life. I understood that waiting for circumstances to change on their own was futile, and it was up to me to take proactive steps towards creating the life I desired.

Through the practice of yoga and meditation, I gained a new perspective on life. It allowed me to rise above my circumstances and view my life from a higher vantage point. It empowered me to take ownership of my own happiness and realize that if I don't make the necessary changes no one else will. Over time, as I began to heal and grow, my psychiatrist was able to taper down the medications I was on and within a period of 4 years I was no longer dependent on medication and becoming a completely new person. This experience made me realize how I was my own worst enemy, running away from happiness and the love of those who cared for me as if something or someone magically would change my life. This gave birth to my entrepreneurial venture Wellness with Sahila in 2019.

Through regular sadhana (6 steps of sadhana mentioned below) we can start rebuilding trust and nurturing the connections that are truly important to us. We also become more aware of how our work and lifestyle choices impact our overall well-being. It is then that we can make conscious decisions, like shifting our career, quitting old habits, if necessary, to realign with our values and priorities.

STEP 4: Discover and eradicate subconscious problems.

This stage is where most of us feel stuck & finding answers seems impossible. It's indeed one of the most challenging phases of our lives. Many individuals either turn to practices such as yoga or seek the guidance of psychologists in search of something more meaningful. I can personally relate to your experience, as I too found solace in yoga when I felt trapped in my own life despite seeing a psychologist and a psychiatrist.

It's interesting how we can have all the external trappings of success - a loving family, a successful career, and financial stability - and yet still find ourselves feeling miserable and devoid of meaning. This realization led me to delve deeper into the practice of yoga, and in doing so, I transcended those surface-level problems. Through this journey, I experienced true bliss and gained a clear understanding of the subconscious issues that were at the root of my discontent.

Let's compare the mental problems to the analogy of a pressure cooker. It's a powerful metaphor that highlights the importance of paying attention to our mental well-being. Just like a pressure cooker, our mental problems act as warning signs, loudly sending whistles signaling that something is amiss within us and that we need help. Life sends us multiple whistles, but if we continually ignore them, the pressure within us will build until it eventually bursts open.

Hence retrospectively speaking, having mental problems can be seen as a positive sign, a wake-up call for us to take charge of our lives and embark on a journey of spiritual growth. It serves as an invitation to look inward and address the root causes of our struggles. Unfortunately, most individuals choose to ignore these signs, leading to further suffering and a continued sense of being stuck. Such individuals find themselves in this helpless state for months to years and this can lead to autoimmune illnesses and cancer. (For more understanding of this please refer to my book- The Why Behind Cancer published in 2023). Unfortunately, only a small 10% understand, pay attention to this whistle or wakeup call and start acting or putting their life together. The remaining 90% remain ignorant or confused. That's when it leads to other kinds of health problems.

How to develop maturity to wake up?

Emotional maturity and intellectual maturity.

Intellectual maturity comes from understanding the human realities of life & emotional maturity comes from developing comfort with those realities.

Throughout life we avoid unhappiness- Our natural inclination is to avoid unhappiness in life. It's true that when someone or something makes us angry, sad, or uncomfortable, our immediate response is often to distance ourselves or try to change the external circumstances to bring about happiness. We yearn for others to behave in a certain way, for relationships to adhere to our expectations, and for our environment to meet our specific preferences. Even my kids insist on a precise temperature range for their room! However, yoga offers a different perspective. It teaches us that constantly striving to control and change the external world can lead to a perpetual struggle. Instead, it encourages us to shift our focus inward and work on ourselves. By redirecting our efforts towards personal growth and self-improvement, we can find a greater sense of peace and fulfillment.

For example- if you cannot stand the smell of coffee and if your partner loves coffee what are the best ways to deal with such a situation. Obviously divorcing your partner because you cannot stand the smell of coffee seems not only ridiculous but an extreme step. Instead, one can try using a room freshener when the smell of coffee bothers you or just focusing your attention elsewhere when coffee is being made like listening to your favorite music and shifting your awareness to something enjoyable can be more reasonable remedies. The same analogy can be applied to a partner who snores loudly at night. There are many such examples where your partner or the environment in which you live cannot be controlled by you all the time.

What is the difference between being alone and feeling lonely?
__Being alone is a choice and feeling lonely is an emotion__.
One is normal and another is abnormal.

Being alone is indeed a choice, a state of being where one can have numerous friends and still enjoy solitude. On the other hand, feeling lonely is an emotion, which can occur even in the midst of a large gathering.

The person who feels lonely often finds themselves constantly striving to change their external environment. They may feel misunderstood by their parents, experience a breakup with a partner, or face overwhelming work demands from their boss. It's understandable that one may desire to change these circumstances, but the reality is that we cannot control or change every person or situation we encounter. If we remain fixated on changing others, we may find ourselves trapped in a cycle of complaint and discontentment.

In contrast, the person who embraces being alone recognizes that they possess everything they want or need within themselves. They understand that true fulfillment comes from within, not from external sources. This individual may be devoted to their spiritual practice, their purpose, and their personal growth. They find joy and fulfillment in their solitude, and they are not afraid to live that way for the rest of their lives. They have their yoga, their purpose, and their spiritual journey to keep them company. For them, this kind of solitude is freedom and liberation.

These are the great yogis, unafraid to meditate alone in the mountains or forests where there is shortage of basic resources like food or clothing. While most of us may not be inclined to spend even a single night in such solitude, we can learn from their example and strive to find contentment and companionship within ourselves. These yogis find joy and fulfillment in their solitude, and they are not afraid to live that way for the rest of their lives.

Chapter 2

Negativity, Fear & Guilt

STEP 5: Stop feeling guilty about the past.

Our subconscious minds are conditioned to certain dogmas or fixed concepts that are deep rooted in our minds since childhood. For example, fear of spiders, hatred for parent/sibling, jealousy of dear friend. This is called conditioning of brain in psychology. You can slowly change them once you are able to recognize these deep-rooted conditions and learn to accept and let go of the negative emotions attached to it.

For some of us forgiving others may seem easier than forgiving one's own self. Because when you realize you have done something wrong to someone or to your own self that's a tough space to be in because that incident or trauma lies in your memory and comes back often like a flashback. How to stop experiencing that negativity repeatedly and how to move on and get the best out of our lives.

4 simple steps to forgive oneself.

1: Realize everyone however good or bad one feels now has done mistakes in their past

When we realize that each one of us has done blunders some small while some big in our past, forgiving ourselves may seem easier. A few of us have experienced traumatic incidents involving someone we love or related to close family members like hurting a parent or spouse or kid. We may have said or done something that hurt them a lot. If possible, talk to the concerned person and express how you feel about hurting him/her and how much you regret it. If the concerned member is not reachable due to death or diseased or unable to trace him/her, then send a simple prayer for that person expressing your sincere apologies and meditate for them for at least 5 minutes. This kind of meditation will bring you peace from within. Any feelings that are expressed authentically will be felt from within.

2: Journal your thoughts

Whenever you go through a phase of guilt or unforgettable shame or humungous amount of regret, you often find your thoughts racing faster than your words. You may find your tongue tied or simply unable to express yourself clearly when confronted with the situation or the person. I have always found that journaling my thoughts first on a piece of paper or even just typing on a word document helps me in consolidating my thoughts in 1 place. I also found journaling a good tool to let out all my true sentiments without polishing it or faking it. This helps me express my thoughts in the rawest manner from my subconscious mind and my conscious mind. After I have written down all my thoughts, I then arrange them in points and try to address each point 1 at a time. This way I have formulated my thoughts and am able to express them in a more organized way to the person who I hurt. I also found that this way of expressing helps avoid unnecessary fights, arguments and further escalation of events. This is particularly important if you intend to mend that relationship for a better future.

3: Promise to give yourself a lot of time

Usually matters concerned with forgiving and forgetting can take a long time. Time is the best healer when it comes to matters of the heart. Having said that there are a few instances where you may not get forgiveness or acceptance from the person you wronged. That does not mean you did the wrong thing by asking for forgiveness. it just means the other person is not ready to move on. He or she is in a different stage in life and has not gone through sufficient maturity or growth to understand your thought processes or actions. That person may never reach a stage or maturity to forgive or forget or even process what they have been through with you. It has nothing to do with your intention to seek forgiveness. For ex- A 7-year-old kid will never forgive his parents for divorcing but when he turns into a parent 30 years later and faces similar situations in life, he may find what his parents did 30 years ago was not so offensive after all. But it took 30 plus years for him to perceive his parents' actions. So, in this case the boy's parents have to learn to forgive themselves for going ahead with the divorce because they wanted to find peace for themselves and believe that time will heal their relationships.

4: Don't dwell in the negative moment

When you have forgiven yourself for a negative action or thought, stop dwelling in that moment for a long time. Most people who say they have forgiven themselves also have the habit of revisiting those painful moments again and again and not realizing that they are dwelling in that moment longer than they should. This merely

prolongs the negative experiences you had and makes it harder to forget. So, learn to train your mind to stop dwelling there any longer and move forward with your life. I found meditation a useful tool to help with this and also to help with all the above steps as well. We will be talking later about ANTAR MOUNA or inner peace to practice strong meditation techniques. Not all stories have to have a happy ending. Sometimes forgiveness means you don't recall negative flashbacks and are able to enjoy the present moment.

STEP 6: Small dissatisfaction is necessary to drive you higher.

Some amount of dissatisfaction is necessary in order to acquire more knowledge, more learning, more hard work, more achievement. Without a sense of purpose or a quest for knowledge, life can indeed become passionless and mundane. Even the Maha yogis, Vedantis, and Rishis, who may appear to be sitting still in meditation, are engaged in a profound pursuit of wisdom, and understanding. Dissatisfaction, in this context, can serve as a catalyst for growth and self-improvement. This kind of dissatisfaction will take you closer to your purpose.

What is the difference between goal and purpose?

1: Goals have specific end points, but purpose is an ongoing phenomenon. such as winning a gold medal in the Olympics, running a full marathon, or achieving financial milestones. They provide short-term motivation and a sense of accomplishment when achieved. However, once we reach these goals, there can be a lingering yearning for more, a hunger to continue striving for something greater. On the other hand, purpose is an ongoing journey without a defined endpoint. Purpose-driven individuals dedicate their lives to a cause or mission that transcends specific achievements or milestones. They create a movement, silently working towards their purpose, knowing that their impact will endure even after they are gone. Movements like "Save Soil" initiated by Sadguru or the principle of **Ahimsa** championed by

Gandhi are examples of purpose-driven endeavors that continue to thrive today.

2: It's true that goal driven people become addicted to the feeling of exhilaration & fulfillment-

Dopamine, epinephrine, and cortisol levels are elevated during moments of accomplishment. The rush of hormones can indeed become addictive, leading individuals to constantly seek that high through the pursuit of new goals or achievements. For example, when someone crosses the finish line of a marathon, they are flooded with a sense of accomplishment, and they may capture this moment through photos on social media or proudly display their medals and certificates. However, once the initial excitement fades, they may find themselves back in the routine of

daily life, where the mundane tasks and responsibilities can create a sense of monotony. This can trigger the desire for another goal or challenge to recreate that rush of endorphins. However, it's essential to recognize that purpose-driven individuals operate on a different wavelength. Rather than seeking temporary highs from accomplishments, they are driven by an ongoing sense of purpose. Their focus is not on the fluctuating levels of endorphins but on the lifelong pursuit of their purpose. This purpose becomes the guiding force in their lives, providing a constant sense of meaning and fulfillment.

3: People who are goal driven impact only themselves

Goal-driven individuals often focus on personal achievements and the well-being of their immediate family members. While their goals may result in personal wealth or power, the broader impact on others may be limited. For instance, someone aiming to become the CEO of a company or earn a significant bonus may primarily benefit themselves and their immediate family. While this can lead to a comfortable and luxurious lifestyle, the impact on others beyond their close circle is minimal unless they consciously choose to donate.

On the other hand, purpose-driven individuals have a profound impact on those they encounter. They go beyond personal achievements and strive to inspire and motivate others. Their purpose is not confined to short-term goals but encompasses a broader mission or cause. An exemplary example is the great **Dalai Lama,** who will always be remembered for his contributions to world peace and joy. His purpose-driven life has touched the lives of countless individuals, spreading wisdom, compassion, and inspiration. His impact extends far beyond himself and his immediate circle, making a significant difference in the world.

4: Goal driven person will be remembered only for a short period.

While the accomplishments of goal-driven individuals may be noteworthy in the moment, they can fade from our minds over time. For example, if asked about the winner of last year's ice-skating gold medalist, many may struggle to recall the name. However, the names of iconic figures like Swami Vivekananda, Martin Luther King resonate with us and are remembered for generations. Their influence and impact extend far beyond their lifetime.

These purpose-driven individuals are rewriting history and reshaping the world through their unwavering commitment to their cause. Their names resurface in conversations and discussions, serving as beacons of inspiration and wisdom. They become immortal not because of personal achievements or fleeting goals, but because they have dedicated their lives to a purpose greater than themselves.

Swami Vivekananda, whose powerful speech in 1893 at the World's Parliament of Religions in Chicago is still remembered by millions. His purpose was not to amass wealth or fame, but to bring authentic yoga and showcase the true essence of India to the West. His legacy lives on, as evidenced by the street named after him in Chicago, serving as a testament to his enduring impact.

STEP 7: Stop comparing yourself to others.

How to feel genuinely happy for others? How to stop comparing yourself to others?

When this attitude goes out of control then at times the comparison leads to an unhealthy level of competition, and you start wishing them ill.

Remember you are not alone. Our society teaches us that success is derived through competition and by pushing others down. This survival-based mentality can create a culture where people feel the need to wish harm upon friends, siblings, or acquaintances to elevate themselves. However, this type of competition is not only unhealthy but also leads to self-destruction in the long run and has pushed many to perform unruly and unjust actions.

We hear acts of violence seen in schools and colleges due to jealousy among students. For example- Bullying your friend in school for getting high likes on IG posts. Ridiculing your colleague for making it to the top faster than his counterparts did. Passing unruly comments on a public figure for gaining fame or victory. For some their entire existence is dependent on this vicious cycle of negativity and targeting people who are more successful than themselves. Our ego derives pleasure by targeting other people's high moments & instead of supporting and uplifting one another, we allow our ego to take control and find satisfaction in the fortune or misfortunes of others.

The genuinely happy people derive happiness not just from their own success but also from the state of gratitude. It comes from a heart centered energy where contentment and satisfaction exist within. In other words, you can be genuinely happy for others only when you are truly happy with yourself. Such a state of mind has an abundance of overflowing joy. Such a person will always imagine and wish only the best for others even when they know the other person may not have his best interest.

On the other hand, people who are inflicted with self-pity or people who are constant complainers can never find genuine happiness for themselves & for others. Their pleasure-seeking attitude gets in the way of their thought processes and interferes with the feeling of joy. It is unfortunate to witness such conflicts and misunderstandings between siblings or friends.

In the case of the two sisters, it seems that the younger sister is concerned about the older sister's health and believes that she should prioritize her well-being over material possessions. On the other hand, the older sister feels that her younger sister is not truly happy for her and is instead harboring feelings of jealousy. This miscommunication and lack of understanding can cause rifts in their relationship. Similarly, in the case of the two male friends, the friend who is earning more money may feel that his friend is not supportive of his success and chooses to exclude him from family events. This exclusion further exacerbates the feelings of resentment and hurt between them. Every now and then we hear of such family feuds and misunderstandings just because we were never taught how to be genuinely happy for others.

Hence, it's disturbing to see many wonderful people who tend to quarrel, judge, and criticize others due to comparisons and competition. This behavior stems from a mindset of separation, where individuals struggle to accept others wholeheartedly. To overcome this, we must unlearn the notion of separation and relearn the essence of oneness, a concept called YAGNA in yoga.

Yagna simply means bringing things together. This cooperative enterprise is called yagna. Examples- Keertan is yagna, Havan is yagna, our Body is perfect example of yagna. A Family is also a perfect example of yagna. Mother earth is also in Yagna all the time.

Truly, as with all complex systems in nature, well-being emerges from coordination – not via competition - between constituent parts. Each component, be it an organ or faculty, serves not for its own glorification but to uplift the whole through synergy. Just as eyes guide feet and hands clear obstacles for smoother passage, so too must mind and body communicate as allies. Only through such cooperation does one thrive; alone, each risks atrophy. Wisdom dawns in realizing no single piece alone forms the miracle that is life.

1: It is crucial to remember that the universe is interconnected, and it never leaves anyone behind. The universe is constantly rooting for each one of us to succeed. Just look at the adoration and support that people have for celebrities. Why do fans cry when their loved ones suffer? Why do people celebrate when their favorite sports stars achieve high scores? It is because we are fully capable of living and enjoying the success stories of others. Don't let your inner spirit wither and become sluggish.

2: How do we stop envying others? The one thing that we all are guilty of doing is envying others for simple monetary pleasures. My friend has this new lipstick, and I don't. My sister has lost a few pounds of weight, and I cannot. My colleague got a huge promotion at work, and I didn't. My brother went to this cool place for vacation, and I can't afford it and so on. Always remember this person who has made you jealous has done nothing to hurt you intentionally. He is just posting or rejoicing his success and everything he or she has done is purely innocent and was not done to target your jealousy or increase your greediness. Everyone is acting from their own levels of ignorance. You may have done something in the past that made another person jealous of you and the world operates in the same way today.

3: How to get over this feeling of constant jealousy? Take risks & don't be afraid to fail and make tough decisions. Don't call yourself names like lazy, idiot, unlucky or stupid even if you're not speaking aloud. You wouldn't want anyone else calling you those names so stop calling yourself names that brings down your confidence. Talk to yourself with empathy and love & be nice to yourself when you fail. Understand that everyone makes mistakes and encounters setbacks. By surrounding yourself with positivity you will slowly overcome the feelings of jealousy.

4: Be mindful of who we turn to for counsel & advice. Especially when making important decisions in our lives. While it is natural to seek the opinions of those close to us, such as family or friends, it is important to consider their level of expertise and experience in the specific area we need guidance in. Asking a parent about whether or not to divorce a partner, for example, may not always yield the most objective or informed advice. Their response may be influenced by their own biases and desires, rather than what is truly best for you. Instead, it is wise to seek advice from individuals who have relevant experience and expertise. Just as you wouldn't ask a doctor for financial investment advice or an attorney for medical advice, it is important to choose your advisors wisely.

5: Learn from your past. Earlier when I used to envy other people it arose from my own insecurities. It arose from my own disappointments or failure to fulfil my goals. Today whenever I catch myself envying others even at the slightest chance I immediately pull back and turn towards myself. Why am I comparing myself to this person? What aspects of their life or achievements am I envious of? What can I learn from this person? What qualities or actions inspire me, and how I can incorporate those lessons into my own life. So eventually as I start to seek more answers from my past my jealousy has now turned into admiration and inspiration for that person. This process of self-reflection, questioning and self-learning comes with practice and maturity and teach this to your younger kids so they can learn the mindset of inspiration rather than envy.

6: Always start with a place of gratitude. Take a moment to admire your partner and your family and your home. When we pause to look around our closets and homes, we often realize the countless blessings we have been bestowed with. This practice of gratitude can provide us with a million reasons to be thankful. It's important to remember that there will always be someone who may appear more beautiful, richer, or more successful than us. However, what truly sets us apart is our uniqueness and individuality. No matter what others may think or say, each of us is special and one-of-a-kind. Each of us possesses something valuable and distinct that no one else can offer or possess.

How do I know that?

Simple, even though there are a billion plus people on planet Earth, no two faces look alike. No genetic makeup looks alike. So, your competition isn't other people. Your competition is your own procrastination & your ego, your unhealthy food that you consume and the knowledge you neglect. Your competition is the negative behavior you're nurturing and your lack of creativity. Now the big question is can you compete against all of that?

- *Can you compete against your own tendencies towards procrastination and replace them with discipline and productivity?*
- *Can you challenge your ego and embrace humility and collaboration?*
- *Can you make healthier choices in your diet and lifestyle and stick with it?*
- *Can you prioritize personal growth and actively seek knowledge?*
- *Can you break free from negative behavior patterns and nurture positive habits?*
- *Can you tap into your creativity and unleash your unique potential?*

Habits you must stop-

- *Never ask someone what their paycheck is.*
- *Never ask someone what their age is.*
- *Never ask someone how much their house or car or possessions are worth.*
- *Never ask someone if they inherited wealth or money.*

STEP 8: Do the work that suits your personality.

It's never too late to reinvent yourself or find a job you love. The notion of talents and what is considered valuable can indeed change over time. What we recognize as talents today may very well evolve or even vanish in the future. For instance, in earlier years in India, individuals who could memorize all the Vedas were hailed as true talents in 12-15th century. However, in today's world, children who can effortlessly memorize the latest Bollywood songs are celebrated for their abilities. This shift is reflective of the changing times and the talents valued by the current generation.

It is crucial to recognize and embrace the special qualities within us, understanding that they may align with the talents and skills valued in the present moment. What brings us joy and fulfillment may not fit into traditional molds or expectations, and that's perfectly alright. The key is to identify those areas where our unique abilities shine and to pursue them wholeheartedly. As the definition of influencers has evolved, we now witness individuals who inspire others through their fashion choices, jewelry, and physical appearance, gaining recognition as influencers. This highlights the importance of adapting to the changing landscape and finding satisfaction in the areas where our talents and passions converge.

10 signs you're in a wrong job or career.

1: You hate going to work and you're disengaged – Many individuals wake up with the feeling in the morning- "Oh My God! I have work today". Instead of waking up with a sense of disappointment or dread about going to work or attending meetings, it's crucial to shift your mindset towards a more positive outlook. Consider reframing your thoughts to focus on the opportunities and possibilities that lie ahead. Ask yourself, "How can I make the most of my time at work today? What can I learn, contribute, or accomplish?"

2: Your unable to relate to your coworkers - It's crucial to establish a strong rapport and connection with your co-workers, as they are not just colleagues, but your teammates. They can be a valuable source of guidance, support, and collaboration. Building positive relationships with your team is essential for a successful and fulfilling work experience. If you find it challenging to relate to your co-workers, it's important to take proactive steps to bridge that gap. Start by trying to get to know them on a personal level. Engage in conversations, ask about their interests, and find common ground.

3: Whole day you find yourself daydreaming/looking for another job - While it's true that many individuals who are unhappy in their current job may find themselves browsing websites for alternative job opportunities or exploring new business ideas, quitting one's job to pursue their passion is not always the immediate or best solution. Before making any drastic decisions, it's important to assess the situation and consider various factors. Ask yourself why you're feeling dissatisfied in your current role. Is it due to a lack of fulfillment, a misalignment with your values, or a toxic work environment? Identifying the root cause can help guide your next steps. If the issue primarily lies with your current job and there are no viable options for growth or improvement, then exploring other opportunities may be worth considering.

4: You wish you could go back and do things differently - It's common to experience moments of reflection and wonder about what could have been if we had made different choices in our lives. While it's natural to have these thoughts, it's important to remember that dwelling on them won't change the present reality. Instead of letting your mind wander to alternate paths, it's crucial to focus on the task at hand and make the most of the opportunities in front of you.

5: You don't feel inspired, challenged, or motivated at work - It's unfortunate to feel uninspired, unchallenged, and unmotivated in your work, especially if you're primarily motivated by the need to pay your bills. Many individuals find themselves in similar situations, where work becomes merely a means to an end, and few may not even realize that they are in such a position because they are too busy working. However, it's important to remember that you have the power to make changes and find a job that brings you both financial stability and fulfillment.

6: Your mental & physical health is suffering- It's unfortunate to hear about the experiences of individuals who wait too long to address their unhappiness and its impact on their health. Delaying action in a job that is draining and causing physical and emotional distress can have serious consequences. Our bodies often give us warning signals when something is not right. Physical symptoms like lack of sleep, back pain, and swollen joints can be manifestations of the stress and unhappiness we experience in an unfulfilling job. It's crucial to take these symptoms seriously and not wait until they escalate into more serious health issues. Our health should always be a top priority, and staying in a job that significantly affects our well-being is not sustainable in the long run. I can't begin to explain how often I see people who ignored these warning signs initially and then come back months or years later with very serious issues like diabetes, depression or even cancer.

7: You have no interest in going up the ladder at work - If you're content with your current position and not interested in climbing the ladder, that's perfectly valid. However, it's important to ensure that you're still challenged and engaged in your work. Seek new projects, take on additional responsibilities, or explore opportunities for professional development that align with your interests and goals.

8: You start underperforming and negative reviews are increasing - When you find yourself disliking your job, it's natural for your performance to be affected. Underperforming can manifest in various ways, such as arriving late, leaving early, missing work-related calls, or taking excessive sick days. These signs serve as indicators that the current job may not be the right fit for you.

9: You feel undervalued or unappreciated- When you find yourself unhappy in your work, it's not uncommon to vent your frustrations and constantly complain about various aspects of your job, such as your boss or the work system. It's natural to seek recognition, appreciation, and quick results, but it's essential to reflect on your own actions and mindset in order to drive positive change. Continuously complaining about your work environment without taking proactive steps to address the issues can perpetuate a cycle of negativity.

10: You don't look up to your seniors at work- When you don't find yourself looking up to your seniors at work, it can be a sign of a disconnect or lack of inspiration within the workplace. It's important to have role models and mentors who can guide and inspire you in your professional journey.

CHAPTER 3

Anger, Hatred and Foul mouth

STEP 9: When we do not forgive others, it changes overtime to hatred.

The path to forgiveness is not easy but it's not impossible either. ***A person with normal physiological condition will not do any wrongdoing. But when a person is under a stressful condition then he/she is capable of wrongdoing.*** If one understands this logic, then forgiveness comes easily. Each one of us is capable of hurting someone or getting hurt by another, which can be your spouse, child, parent, relative, colleague or friend or someone unrelated. When you don't forgive someone, it slowly overtimes changes into anger or hatred or violence etc. That's the reason we hear gun shootings almost every day in public places. So here are 5 steps to forgive someone-

1-DDD-Decompose, detach it and don't attempt to understand

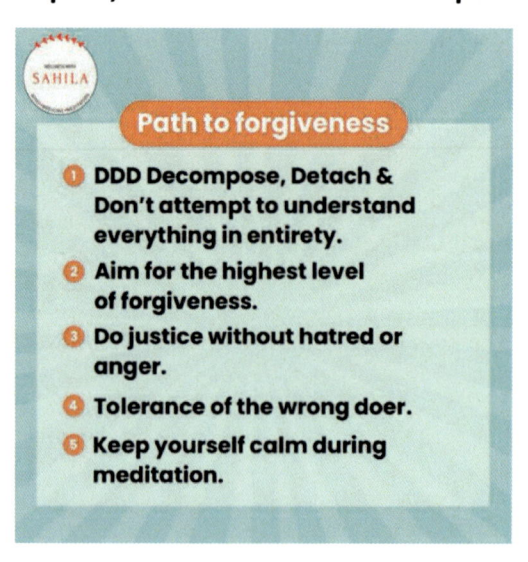

Path to forgiveness
1. DDD Decompose, Detach & Don't attempt to understand everything in entirety.
2. Aim for the highest level of forgiveness.
3. Do justice without hatred or anger.
4. Tolerance of the wrong doer.
5. Keep yourself calm during meditation.

everything in entirety. Forgiveness is not forgetting. When we forget what we do it's still embedded in our subconscious brain, and it resurfaces whenever there is slight trigger. For ex. Girl who has been raped as a child may assume she has forgotten the event, but whenever she watches or reads a rape event the flashbacks come back to her and bothers her again. Hence It becomes necessary to decompose and detach the painful event in stages. In this case the same girl will understand the rape differently at age 10, differently at age 20 and differently at age 30. And even though the event may have occurred months or years ago it's impossible to understand everything that happened to her on that day 1. It's advisable to do it in stages and remember it takes time to regress from that situation and accept it.

Sometimes the healing can take years and that's ok because different people process the information differently. But make a conscious effort to decompose and detach from the pain slowly rather than living with it your entire life. Living with the memory of pain is more painful for you than for the person who caused it in first place because studies shows that it leads to psychological illnesses like post-traumatic stress disorders (PTSD) very commonly seen in rape and abuse victims and war victims.

2-**Aim for the highest level of forgiveness –which is not to develop any ill feeling towards the wrong doer**. This is toughest but gives you permanent results and relaxes your mind. Again, meditation is the key and read books written by Dalai Lama especially one that touched me deeply was – The Book of Joy where he explains the joy of living a life that is pain free with no hatred or resentment against anyone. This state is truly a blissful state, and one needs to experience this in order to understand the importance of forgiving someone.

3-**Next level of forgiving is to do justice without hatred or anger**.

This can transform our attitude towards that person who wronged you in the first place. Most women historically whether ancient days Draupadi or modern-day Royal family princess Diana, they showed us how they transformed their anger and hatred against the wrong doer by helping other women who faced similar struggles. This leads to a more constructive method of healing and forgiving rather than living with hatred for the rest of your lives. It also allows one to reach a higher level in philanthropy where you can support, teach, and guide other people who are suffering like you and what better way to heal than heal in a group. This is also the basis for modern day group therapy commonly used in alcohol addicts, anger management, depression etc. Discussing the problem in a group who have undergone a similar set of distress helps us cope better and allows us to be brutally honest with our feelings. I plan to start **Chakra Anonymous** group discussions this year during summer where the participants can hide their identity & yet share their concerns particularly traumas that occurred in their past lives. I will be the moderator to help navigate their traumas constructively into acceptance and forgiveness.

4-**Next level is tolerance of the wrong doer and that shows your inner strength.** Even if the person who caused you pain is in front of you as in case your spouse, family member or neighbor, please attempt to stay strong without showing your anger or resentment. This may be tough if the person who hurts you stays with you all the time. This is usually the case between mother-in-law and daughter-in-law fights, or the most common situation seen between a husband & wife. Shockingly in some cases I see people are in hatred with each other so much so that they plan to kill each other either by poisoning the food or pushing them from their balcony etc. By acting on your hatred you are merely inviting more problems into your life like crime investigation, anxiety, OCD (obsessive compulsive disorder) etc. This further aggravates your stress and puts you in an elevated category of psychosocial stresses.

5-**Last crucial step to keep ourselves calm by meditation-** this step is crucial for incorporating all the above 4 steps and becomes the foundation of forgiveness. Among the above 4 steps one can skip or go back and forth but in order to effectively do any of the above steps you need to practice meditation. When you develop forgiveness for the person who caused you pain you automatically go to an elevated state of gratitude. As I have mentioned before multiple times, gratitude is the beginning of spiritual realization. Meditation allows one to reach that state effortlessly and with ease. That is why every class of my yoga or chakra healing will include meditation or rather guided group meditation to take you into that mode of elevated level by cleaning your thoughts and emotions.

Step 10-Avoid these 4 things while conversing with people.

The way we speak can uplift or destroy people. Gandhi spoke in such a way so as to uplift people. Hitler spoke in a way that would destroy people. Truth is not limited to speech alone. Truth or

4 things to avoid while conversing with others

1. Abuse & Obscenity
2. Dealing in falsehoods
3. Calumny or telling tales.
4. Ridiculing others beliefs & faiths.

Satya comes from our thoughts, our speech and finally action. So, our words carry immense power and at times we fail to recognize that power which is the main cause of relationship problems today.

1-Abuse and obscenity. It is true that curse words have become increasingly prevalent in today's society, appearing in the language used by adults, in movies, songs, and even on social media. This normalization of cursing can have unintended consequences, particularly when it comes to the influence it has on children. Children are highly impressionable, and exposure to cursing at a young age can lead them to mimic these behaviors. As responsible adults, it is crucial to set a positive example and create an environment where cursing is not tolerated or encouraged. One way to promote a more positive language is by addressing the word "hate." While it may not be considered a traditional curse word, it carries a strong negative connotation. Encouraging children (and ourselves) to replace the word "hate" with "I don't like" can help foster a more compassionate and understanding mindset. To put this idea to the test, I encourage you to count how many times you use the word "hate" on a daily basis.

- *I hate coffee.*
- *I hate winter.*
- *I hate my boss.*
- *I hate this movie and the list goes on.*

My personal experience with my mother's use of obscene language highlights the importance of mindful and respectful communication, particularly within the family dynamic. It's unfortunate that my mother grew up without proper guidance or correction regarding her language usage. The absence of positive role models and the lack of attention during her upbringing contributed to her habitual use of curse words. The fact that my mother directed curse words towards me, from a young age almost on a daily basis is deeply saddening. Hurtful words can have a profound impact on a child's self-esteem and emotional well-being. The loss of my mother's ability to speak due to her brain cancer serves as a poignant reminder of the importance of cherishing our words and using them responsibly. It's a powerful lesson in the impact our words can have, and a call to prioritize kindness, empathy, and understanding in our interactions with others. Today she can speak only as less as 2 words despite all treatment and therapy. Let us all be mindful of the power of our words and strive to create an environment where our communication brings joy, healing, and positivity.

Today we often see young kids as young as 5 years using curse words at one another and it's most picked up from their parents who yell or curse each other during their arguments and fights. Thereby parents unfortunately are creating a toxic environment for their little ones and this toxicity is deeply engrained in their kids' minds.

2-Dealing in falsehoods- It's disheartening to see how some individuals resort to dishonesty in order to make profits, especially when it comes to selling goods through false claims and misleading advertisements. This kind of business practice not only harms others but also invites negative consequences for oneself in the form of bad karma. As someone who values integrity and the trust of my followers and friends, I refused to entertain such commercials on my social media page. By staying true to my principles and refraining from promoting falsehoods, I want to maintain the trust my listeners and followers have placed in me. Remember, the choices we make in business and in life have consequences. By staying true to your values and refusing to engage in dishonest practices, you are aligning yourself with positive karma and creating a more ethical and trustworthy environment for yourself and those around you. Hence my social media platform serves as a channel for promoting wellness and providing valuable insights to my audience.

3-Calumny or telling tales- It's unfortunate that gossiping about others has become a prevalent and harmful behavior, particularly among women. Engaging in gossip and spreading rumors can have serious consequences, causing rifts between friends, couples, and even within families. It's essential for people to recognize the negative impact gossiping can have and make a conscious effort to refrain from participating in such behavior. Gossiping not only wastes valuable time and energy, but it also damages relationships and can have long-lasting repercussions. Instead of indulging in gossip, let's focus our time and energy on building positive and meaningful connections with others. Engage in conversations that uplift, inspire, and foster understanding. Seek to empathize with others rather than judge or criticize them based on hearsay.

4-Ridiculing others' beliefs and faiths- It is crucial to exercise caution when attempting to be humorous or make fun of others. We must ensure that our words and actions do not undermine or hurt their beliefs and faiths in any way. I have personally witnessed the negative impact that insensitivity and ridicule can have on individuals and their relationships, and it is a lesson worth sharing. I recall an experience with a close friend who held strong opposition towards tattoos. She adamantly expressed that she would never permit her children to get one. When I revealed my tattoo of Lord Ganesha, she couldn't fathom how someone like me, a doctor, could allow such an adornment on my body. Despite my explanation that Lord Ganesha holds a special place in my heart (my Ishta Devatha), and having the tattoo was a way to keep him close, she remained dismissive. Unfortunately, my friend chose to ridicule my tattoo whenever we were in a group setting. She went so far as to expose my body part forcefully to others and make vulgar jokes about it. This behavior caused me significant pain, but I chose to remain silent, recognizing her ignorance and inability to understand the importance of others' faith and beliefs. It is essential to emphasize the significance of respecting the beliefs and faiths of others before engaging in ridicule or mockery. We must recognize that these aspects hold deep meaning and personal significance to individuals, and it is not our place to undermine or belittle them.

Effective & inoffensive communication is very important to keep your relationships strong and joyful. Also most importantly don't invite bad karma onto yourself. Because what you think, you speak, and what you speak can leave repercussions in your future.

STEP 11-Learn to first relax yourself.

Our bodies were indeed designed for movement, while our minds were designed to find stillness and focus. However, in today's urban societies, many of us practice the opposite. This means we have fallen into the trap of constantly being connected to Wi-Fi and glued to our electronic devices. This nonstop connection has become so ingrained in our lives that we feel disabled or anxious when we are without it, even for a brief moment. Undoubtedly, the internet and modern technology have revolutionized the way we work and communicate, allowing us to be more efficient and productive. However, in the process, we have unintentionally become sedentary, confined to a single position for prolonged periods as we immerse ourselves in our laptops or smartphones. This lack of movement has significant implications for our physical and mental well-being. Our bodies crave and require regular physical activity to function optimally. When we neglect this need and remain stagnant, we may experience distress, unhappiness, and a host of health issues.

This brings us to the second half of the equation— our minds are supposed to stay still but almost all the time our minds are thinking constantly, and this destroys our peace of mind. **Why is constant thinking bad?** When our minds are constantly preoccupied with an incessant stream of thoughts, it becomes challenging to think clearly and stay focused on our goals. This lack of focus and mental clarity can drain our energy and leave us feeling exhausted. The effects of an overactive mind manifest in various ways. The workload keeps piling up, and we may experience physical discomfort such as body aches and headaches. Sleep becomes elusive, and even when we do manage to rest, we wake up feeling fatigued, with a reluctance to engage in further activities. These signs indicate that our minds are overworked and in need of respite. By engaging in meditation, we create space for our minds to settle and find stillness. Through meditation, we can observe and detach from the constant stream of thoughts, allowing our minds to rest and recharge.

So here are **Six stages of Antar Mouna** to be followed in same hierarchy starting with step 1 onwards. For those who are new to meditation you may need to practice step 1 and 2 for many months and reaching the last step may take a few years too. In

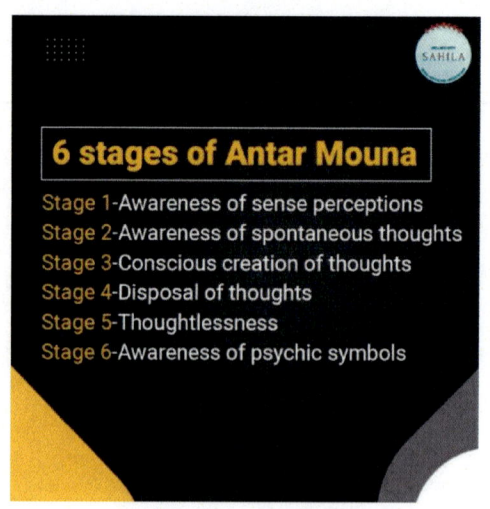

6 stages of Antar Mouna

Stage 1-Awareness of sense perceptions
Stage 2-Awareness of spontaneous thoughts
Stage 3-Conscious creation of thoughts
Stage 4-Disposal of thoughts
Stage 5-Thoughtlessness
Stage 6-Awareness of psychic symbols

other words, the goal is not to reach the final step hurriedly but to indulge in each step slowly and try to assimilate them by daily sadhana.

Stage 1-**Awareness of sense perceptions**-

Become more aware of the external sounds, people around you, listen to the sounds of rainwater outside, buzzing bees etc. In this stage you intentionally direct your perception to the outside world. Here you become intensely aware of all the 5 sense organs. Once you become aware of everything happening around you then you lead to stage 2. From extroversion you become introverted. Stop focusing on other people around you and focus on sense perceptions and from there direct the focus onto yourself. From intentional awareness of the outside world, you go into introversion in stage 2. From outside perception slowly you go into becoming the seer or the observer. In yoga we call this **drashta or seer.**

Discard all judgements, criticisms, or emotions. If you hear your phone ring while in stage 1, don't judge or say **oh no, why is he calling now?** Simply be aware of the phone ringing. It's not necessary to answer the phone. So, once you become aware of the external perceptions then focus on your breath. Keep doing this phenomenon alternating between external perception and breath control. Become fully aware of the sense organs and yet don't let the emotions overpower you.

Stage 2- **Awareness of spontaneous thoughts**.

Here you become aware of the spontaneous thoughts that arise from our subconscious mind. Whether its fear, or lack of confidence, jealousy, or admiration, whether its negative or positive thoughts, don't suppress it, instead just become fully aware of it. In life we accumulate a vast majority of negative thoughts which have led to unhappiness, chaos, and tension. This stage is called **shankha prakshalana** in yoga. You may relive childhood memories that are hard to forget. You may relive an incident that occurred in your life that you are not very proud of. And so on.

Don't choose positive over negative, just let all thoughts come over to your mind one after the other. Tell yourself that I'm fully aware of this thought but these thoughts are not me, they don't define me, and they don't determine my life's happiness or sadness in any way. Let all kinds of thoughts flow in your mind like a river.

Stage 3- Conscious creation of thoughts

This stage is opposite of stage 2, meaning don't allow spontaneous thoughts instead choose a thought at your will, reflect on it sometime and then throw it out. Be watchful and try not to spend no more than a few minutes on 1 thought. If you're dwelling on it for half an hour, then that becomes stressful, and this is how people invite stress. So, this stage helps create a space in front of your eyes or screen called **chidaksha.** After some time, you become aware of that chidaksha and decide to let it go.

Now choose another thought. Let's say you fear that you will lose your job. After dwelling on that thought for a while, next you reject the idea. Now let the next thought appear and this process is repeated with numerous thoughts one after the other so thoughts from the sub conscious mind is brought to conscious awareness.

Stage 4- **Disposal of thoughts**-

In this stage, thoughts which you have no control over or no way to change them can be let go. This way you will consciously learn to let go of the thoughts that arise and reject.

Allow spontaneous eruption of thoughts.
Choose 1 thought that is deeply buried in your mind.
Reflect on it for some time.
Willfully dispose of it.

So here instead of consciously creating a thought you allow deep thoughts buried in your sub conscious mind to stir up to your conscious mind, become witness to the thought.

Remember, at times you may feel intense emotions like crying or outbursts of anger or extreme fear and yet choose to become a witness to your emotions too. This eventually leads to stage 5. For some, reaching this stage can take up to a few years or months of practice. This is normal and hence do not be in a rush to reach a certain stage.

Stage 5- **Thoughtlessness**

Here after rejecting the unwanted thoughts, the mind finally becomes peaceful and calm. Thoughts can still come and go but they will not be very intense or emotional. Slowly it will lead to the stage of no thoughts or thoughtlessness. For some it may take years to reach this stage of thoughtlessness and yet this is where one can start to feel the powers of meditation. To understand more you can enroll in my daily meditation classes which are conducted for FREE.

Stage 6-**Awareness of psychic symbols**

Each stage requires mastering for few weeks or months and do not jump prematurely into stage 6. Stage 6 is being reserved for only advanced meditators or someone whose Darpak kapha is extremely high. (Darpak is one of the pancha kapha, an element produced in mind). Most Buddhist monks and Hindu saints and Maharishis will begin to see symbols, colors of chakras or even their ishtadevatha. For some it may seem like a light at Agna chakra. The best time to practice antar mouna meditation is early morning when you wake up or before sleep when it's quiet and your mind is calm. The best position is to practice in sukhasana, padmasana, siddhasana or vajrasana. In every stage practice being a witness only. Meaning be alert to all the mind processes but without being involved. In other words, become a detached observer.

Chapter 4

The Human MIND

STEP 12- 5 states of mind

Before delving into the five states of mind, it is important to understand the three types of personalities that exist within us as human beings. Overall, individuals possess three primary types of personalities: **tamasic**, **rajasic**, and **sattvic.**

A tamasic personality is characterized by a sense of dullness and lethargy. This type of person tends to lack enthusiasm and may not be someone that others are eager to spend time with.

On the other hand, a rajasic personality exudes energy and enthusiasm. These individuals are often cheerful and highly focused on pursuing pleasures and desires. In modern terms, we might refer to them as consumers. It is worth noting that most people in today's world tend to possess a rajasic nature.

Lastly, there is the sattvic personality, which represents individuals who have relinquished many worldly pleasures and are moving towards a state of Samadhi, or deep spiritual absorption. These individuals prioritize inner peace, clarity, and higher consciousness.

In most individuals, one of these qualities predominates over the others, influencing their overall disposition and approach to life. Understanding these personality types can provide valuable insights into our own behaviors, tendencies, and aspirations.

1-Ksipta state

The distracted mind, also known as the lowest state of mind, is characterized by thoughts that are scattered and in disarray. It is often referred to as the "monkey mind" because it constantly jumps from one thought to another, leaving a lack of clarity and focus. Individuals with a rajasic nature, who are inclined towards seeking quick pleasures and gratification, often find themselves in this state of mind. For example- people who spend lot of time on social media shopping. Unfortunately, those who consistently experience a distracted mind may also be more susceptible to conditions such as anxiety, bipolar disorder, ADHD, personality disorders, and addictions.

2-Mudha state

The infatuated mind represents a state where individuals are prone to committing violent or unrighteous actions, as well as engaging in unpredictable behavior. This state is often associated with a tamasic or dull nature, where the flow of information to the brain is hindered. Despite being engaged in various activities, individuals with an infatuated mind may feel numb internally, as if the entire universe is working against them.

These individuals may come across as foolish or apathetic, as their thoughts and actions are influenced by a distorted perception of reality. Examples of situations, include person being confined in a prison environment or someone experiencing the depths of depression, divorce, or the death of a loved one. It is important to approach individuals with an infatuated mind with empathy and understanding, recognizing that they are in a vulnerable state. They may require professional assistance and support to navigate their circumstances and regain a sense of equilibrium.

3-Viksipta state

The occasionally steady mind. is filled with numerous thought processes, and the individual is highly energetic. They constantly feel the desire to pursue multiple activities and may find themselves torn between different options, wondering which one to prioritize. While they possess the capacity to accomplish a great deal, their thoughts are not controlled or consolidated.

This personality is predominantly rajasic, characterized by a focus on seeking pleasure and gratification. However, there are occasional influences of sattva, which represent qualities such as clarity and higher consciousness. Individuals in this state may exhibit behaviors such as a young and bright financial analyst investing his money in multiple projects simultaneously or a college student who indulges in partying and dating multiple individuals concurrently. It is important to recognize that this mindset, driven by a desire for pleasure and avoidance of painful situations, is prevalent in most of the population today.

4-Ekagra state

The one-pointed mind- is characterized by a person's ability to focus on a single thing with ease. This state of mind is predominantly in the sattva state, occasionally influenced by rajasic tendencies. It is marked by attentiveness and the ability to achieve a state of one-pointedness. Individuals with a one-pointed mind experience a deep sense of relaxation and focus. They are able to direct their attention towards a specific goal or purpose and align all their activities towards its achievement. This state is often associated with the feeling one gets after a meditation class or the refreshing sensation following a good night's sleep.

Those with a one-pointed mind typically possess high intellectual powers and are driven by their goals. However, it is essential to recognize that the ego can play a significant role in this state. This is where bhakti, or devotion, becomes crucial in controlling the ego. Without the presence of bhakti in the state of **ekagra** (one-pointedness), individuals may become extremely egotistical or introverted. They may feel a strong inclination to distance themselves from others, perceiving them as unintelligent or unworthy of their time and attention.

5-Nirudha state

The restrained mind. - here the individuals are not easily swayed by random thoughts or distress. All three levels of the mind - manas (mind), buddhi (intellect), and ego (ahankara) - are restrained. The concept of "I" or "mine" is completely dissolved across these levels. A person in this state is fully focused on achieving a higher goal, exemplified by great individuals like Gandhi and Buddha. They demonstrate unwavering dedication and commitment to their purpose, transcending personal desires and attachments.

The highest meditative state for a practitioner on the path of sadhana is known as nirudha. From this stage, one can attain samadhi, a state of profound absorption and union with the divine. Individuals on the path of sadhana are called sadhakas. They embark on a journey of self-discovery, seeking spiritual growth and self-realization.

The first 3 states of mind, which is Ksipta, Mudha and Viksipta cannot achieve yoga or meditation and their states of mind make them unfit for yoga. You can advise them every day or send them

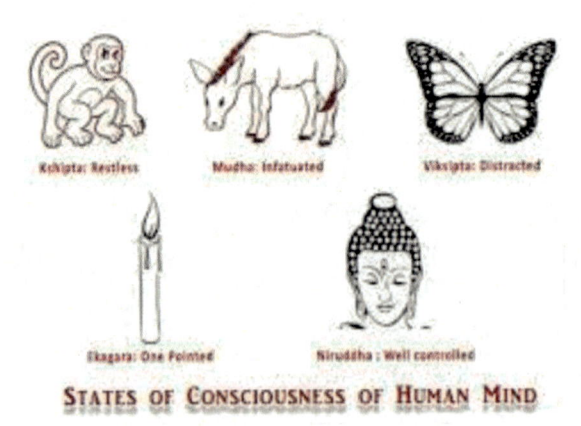

Kshipta: Restless Mudha: Infatuated Viksipta: Distracted

Ekagara: One Pointed Niruddha: Well controlled

STATES OF CONSCIOUSNESS OF HUMAN MIND

reminders daily and yet they will make excuses or refuse to settle in relaxation. Only the last 2 states of mind are conducive to yoga and meditation.

STEP 13: Live totally in the now

Our mind is a reservoir of samskaras or imprints of the past. Most people who suffer from depression or anxiety are continually living in the past, meaning they are overwhelmed with guilt, regret, remorse etc. Sometimes these feelings are deeply imprinted in your memory, and you may not even recognize those emotions in the beginning, and it may be difficult to remove. But we all must start somewhere. We must learn to live in the present. In other words, **we suffer due to our mind and not due to our situations.**

There is indeed a significant distinction between yoga psychology and modern psychology. In the realm of medical psychology or therapy, the focus often lies in finding quick solutions to address specific situations. For instance, if someone is feeling low, they may be prescribed medication, or if they are feeling high, alternative strategies may be suggested. It is important to note that I do not place blame on medical professionals for this approach. Training the mind is a complex phenomenon and a time-consuming process that requires significant investment. Both the patient and the doctor often seek immediate relief, and the luxury of time is not always available.

Yoga psychology, on the other hand, takes a different approach. It delves deep into the root cause of suffering rather than merely addressing surface-level symptoms. The practice of yoga has always emphasized the importance of training the mind and aims to eliminate the underlying causes of problems. It recognizes that true healing and transformation require a comprehensive understanding of the mind-body connection. Hence Yoga psychology encourages individuals to embark on a journey of self-discovery, self-awareness, and self-transcendence.

Yoga sutras written by Patanjali (considered as Father of yoga) has done extensive study of human mind and its thought processes. He has classified human thoughts as follows.

- *5 vrittis or mental fluctuations-pramana, vikalpa, viparyaya, smruti, nidra*
- *5 kleshas or impurities in thoughts-avidya, asmita, raga, dwesha, abhinivesha*
- *12 vikshepas/ vignanas/ vitarkas or obstacles/disturbances to attaining wisdom.*

There are **5 basic vrittis or mental fluctuations** that we often engage in are the main cause of stress. Chitta Vritti Nirodha meaning to stop all the mental fluctuations becomes the basis of yoga sutras and Patanjali goes into the extreme depth of explaining where those mental fluctuations arise and how to stop those mental fluctuations from stealing your mental peace.

Now it's essential to become familiarized with the concept of witness or Sakshi. This is best explained by this example- When I'm going for an evening walk and I begin to admire the sunset, for few moments I get absorbed in the act of observing and momentarily forget my own self. So now there are only 2 components to being a witness, **the act of observing** and the **object being observed.** This is indeed a moment of bliss or joy. It's a state of being fully present and engaged with the beauty of the sunset, without the intrusion of self-consciousness or other distractions. This type of experience is often associated with a sense of awe, wonder, and deep appreciation.

But in today's world, after the first few moments of awe, I always try to bring ME, MYSELF and MY EGO into the picture. It is true that in today's digital age, many people have developed a habit of capturing and sharing their experiences on social media platforms to seek validation and recognition in the form of likes, comments, and shares.

While there's nothing inherently wrong with wanting to share moments of beauty or joy with others, it's worth reflecting on our motivations and the potential impact this behavior may have on our overall experience. Sometimes, the act of constantly reaching for our phones and focusing on capturing the perfect photo or sharing it online in a certain way after filters, can detract from being fully present in the moment and appreciating the experience for its own sake. In other words, I'm no longer a witness to the event because I have added the third component to this which is the **observer.**

Patanjali explains how to avoid these vrittis by first helping us understand what the 5 types of vrittis or mental fluctuations are.

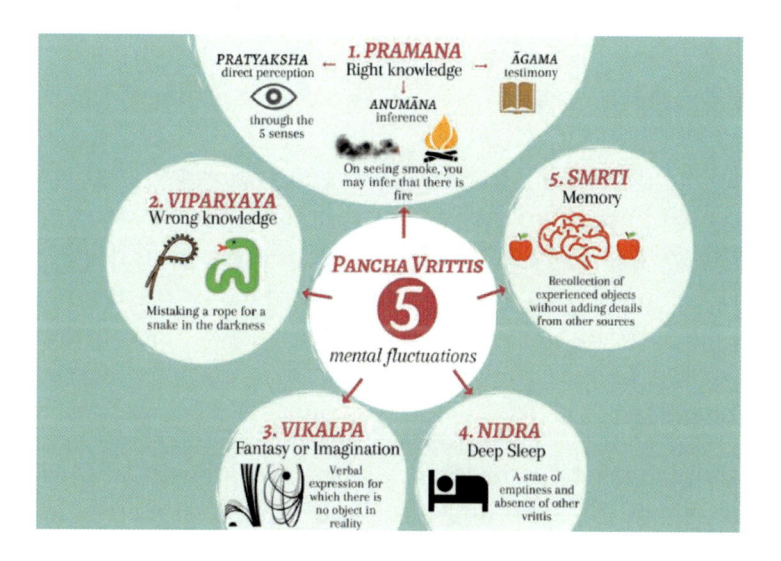

1-Pramana-(Right Knowledge)- the concept of right perception, plays a crucial role in understanding truth or facts as perceived by our 5 sense organs. It holds a significant place in the hierarchy of perception. There are three types of Pramana:

Pratyaksha Pramana: This type of perception involves directly experiencing something through our sense organs. For example, when you are speaking with someone on the phone who claims it is snowing outside, and you look out of your window to see the snow, which is pratyaksha Pramana. It is the first and most reliable, immediate form of perception.

Anumana Pramana: In this type of perception, we derive inferences or suspicions based on the evidence presented to our senses. For instance, if you see smoke from a distance, you may infer that there is a fire, or something has caught fire. This is anumana or a suspicion. While it relies on our senses, it involves making deductions and drawing conclusions based on the evidence at hand. You are still using the sense organs of smell and vision to perceive that there is smoke yet not set eyes directly on the smoke.

Agama Pramana: Agama refers to knowledge gained through authoritative texts or scriptures. When we read something in a book and understand it to be true, it is considered agama Pramana. For example, the Earth is round or that the sun sets in the west are known facts provided in our books. Even if we haven't personally observed these phenomena by measuring the planet or following the sun every minute, we rely on information from trusted sources and make conclusive inferences based on that knowledge.

Both anumana and agama involve perceiving indirect truth. We use our senses to gather information, analyze it, and arrive at conclusions or beliefs. While pratyaksha provides direct perception, anumana and agama involves expanding our understanding beyond what is immediately available to our senses. When in doubt about your thoughts, it is indeed helpful to go back to the basics and rely on the fundamental principles of perception. By utilizing your senses or pratyaksha, you can directly perceive the facts and gather information from your immediate surroundings. This direct experience serves as a reliable source of knowledge.

Now that you have sufficient understanding of what is the correct perception of your sense organs, Patanjali goes onto explain how to use those perceptions intelligently.

What is Apara & Para Pratyaksha?

Within the realm of **pratyaksha** or direct perception, there are two distinct forms: conventional perception or **apara pratyaksha**, and supernormal perception or **para pratyaksha**. Advanced yogis have the ability to acquire knowledge through both of these methods.

Apara Pratyaksha or Conventional knowledge are normal simple facts which are accessible to all, via our sense organs. It is the information we gather from our direct sensory experiences of the world. This is the foundation of our everyday understanding and basic awareness. However, there are occasions when we may feel or perceive something that goes beyond our ordinary five sense organs. This is what is known as supernormal perception or **Para pratyaksha.** It involves perceiving and experiencing phenomena that transcend conventional perception. This form of perception opens new horizons and expands our understanding of reality.

I had a personal experience where, for a period of one year, I felt in touch with your father's soul after his passing. During this time, his presence and advice went beyond normal perception, providing me with guidance and understanding of my mind and body. This experience allowed me to tap into a supernormal form of perception which led me to discover wellness with Sahila in future. Experiences like these can be profound and transformative, offering insights and guidance that can shape our lives. They remind us of the vastness of human consciousness and the potential for deeper connections and understandings.

Now for the sake of understanding we need to differentiate Apara pratyaksha (supernormal perception) with abnormal perception seen in hallucinations. Hallucinations are a common phenomenon seen in certain illnesses like Schizophrenia, bipolar, depression etc. Let us assume for a moment that my interaction with my father after his death were abnormal perception or part of hallucinations then here are some ways it stood apart and clearly indicating to me that its part of apara pratyaksha.

My communication with my father lasted exactly for a period of a year after his death and not a single day longer. All of the things that my father shared with me during that period came out true. They magically disappeared after the 1-year period, which he had mentioned clearly at the beginning of our communication, and I have never communicated with my father ever since in the last 9 years. In other words, such experiences with apara pratyaksha are usually life changing and I thank God and my father every single day for protecting me during that 1 year. If it was not for his guidance, I may not have had the intuition to write this book in the first place or even understand what pratyaksha meant.

What is Abahya & Bahya Pratyaksha?

Yoga also teaches us to recognize and differentiate between internal perception, known as **Abahya pratyaksha** and external perception, known as **Bahya pratyaksha**. These two forms of perception offer different perspectives on a given situation or interaction.

External perception or **Bahya perception** refers to the interpretation of events and actions based on what is visible or observable to our senses. For example, if someone attends your birthday party and presents you with an extravagant gift like a diamond necklace, the external perception would be that they love and admire you. This interpretation is shared by you and your family, as everyone is pleased and excited by the gesture.

On the other hand, internal perception or **Abhaya perception** allows us to tap into our intuition, inner vision, or what some may call a "gut feeling." In the above scenario, what we just witnessed, the person gifting the necklace can also have ill intentions hidden behind the act of giving the necklace. That person is possibly wishing you ill luck or has future hope to acquire a profit or major asset from your business. It provides a deeper understanding of the person's true internal perception, which may not align with the external perception. **Pramana or the right knowledge** in this scenario reminds us not to solely rely on what our eyes see but to perceive and interpret situations with our internal eyes as well. By tapping into our intuition, we can gain insights beyond the surface level and make more informed judgments about people and situations.

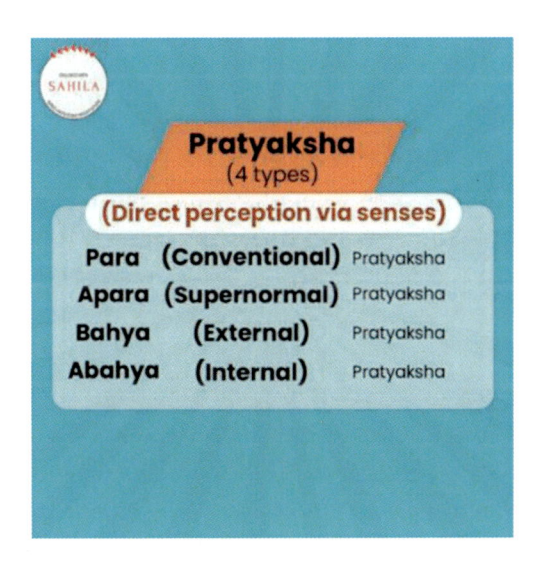

Pratyaksha
(4 types)
(Direct perception via senses)
Para (Conventional) Pratyaksha
Apara (Supernormal) Pratyaksha
Bahya (External) Pratyaksha
Abahya (Internal) Pratyaksha

2-Vikalpa (imaginary perception)-

Metaphors play a significant role in language and communication.

They allow us to convey concepts and ideas in a more vivid and imaginative way. Metaphors such as a flying elephant, talking cow, or the phrase "time flies" add color and depth to our expressions. Even seemingly straightforward statements, such as "the sun rises and sets," are metaphors. In reality, the sun remains stationary, and it is the Earth's rotation that gives the illusion of the sun's movement. However, we commonly use this metaphorical expression without considering the literal truth behind it. It has become a part of our everyday language and understanding.

In this context, it is essential to differentiate between vikalpa and viparyaya. Vikalpa refers to the creation of meaningful expressions that have no physical reality. It allows us to use metaphors and figurative language to convey ideas effectively. There is no error in judgment here, as in the case of viparyaya.

3-Viparyaya (wrong perception or Misunderstanding)-

Distinction between surface-level errors in perception, such as mistaking a rope for a snake, or experiencing double vision after consuming alcohol is known as **viparyaya**. This must be distinguished from the deeper errors in judgment known as **kleshas**. (discussed in pancha klesha in next chapter). In other words, **viparyaya** refers to incorrect perception or erroneous views. It is when our understanding deviates from reality. **Viparyaya** can lead to distorted perceptions and judgments about individuals or events. **Kleshas** are the obstacles or afflictions that cloud our understanding and lead to suffering. For example- different groups of people may have contrasting opinions about Gandhi, with some worshiping him like a deity and others harboring deep resentment towards him as well as blaming him for dividing the country. The debate about which group is in the realm of **kleshas** and which group is in the **viparyaya** revolves around their level of **pramana** or right knowledge each group has about Gandhi.

This analogy can be applied when 2 religious' groups of people argue, or 2 political groups of people argue. Even for an individual to make a **well-informed** decision it becomes necessary to use the above methods, especially crucial decisions like marriage or career choices. However, in any case it is essential to approach this debate with open-mindedness and respect for differing perspectives.

4-Nidra (deep sleep)-

in Patanjali's teachings regarding vritti, which refers to the fluctuations or modifications of the mind, deep sleep is also one. While in this context, pramana, viparyaya, and vikalpa may not directly apply, the absence of these thoughts does contribute to the state of vritti. When we wake up from deep sleep, we can assess the quality of our sleep based on our mental state upon awakening. This demonstrates how our mental state during the later part of the day can be influenced by the nature of our sleep. If we had a restful and rejuvenating sleep, our mental fluctuations may be minimal.

However, if our sleep was disturbed or if we experienced sleep deprivation, it could lead to increased mental fluctuations or vrittis throughout the day. This state of vritti of deep sleep is significant in the practice of yoga because it impacts our overall well-being and state of mind. By understanding the connection between our sleep, mental fluctuations, and daily life, we can become more aware of the factors that affect our mental state and take steps to cultivate balance and stability.

Role of tamas, rajas, and sattva in deep sleep.

In deep dreamless NREM sleep, a person may experience a sense of darkness and often cannot recall their dreams, simply stating that they slept well. This state of deep sleep can indicate a sattvic state of mind. This also essentially achieves a state of chittha vritti nirodha state (this is the first and most used yoga sutra today and essentially means cessation of all mental fluctuations state). Patanjali does mention that this way of deep sleep is tamasic way of experiencing chitta vritti nirodha and must not be considered the highest state. The sattvic way of experiencing chitta vritti nirodha is attained in samadhi, where the yogi is fully awake and lucid to the nature of reality.

Tamas is associated with inertia, darkness, and dullness, while rajas represent activity, restlessness, and passion. A dreamy sleep REM sleep, where one can recall their dreams, may indicate a stronger influence of rajasic or tamasic qualities. When rajas is predominant, one may feel like they have slept restlessly, as seen in conditions like restless legs syndrome. This restlessness can lead to a sense of unease and fatigue upon waking. On the other hand, when tamas is predominant, one may wake up feeling sluggish and tired. This can be observed in situations such as depression, where feelings of lethargy and body aches, particularly shoulder pain or back pain, are evident.

In contrast, when sattva is predominant, the quality of sleep is enhanced, resulting in a refreshed and recharged feeling upon waking. This is the kind of experience I have now with my sleep state. Even with fewer hours of sleep (compared to 10 years ago when I was depressed), waking up naturally during brahma muhurta before 5:30 am and feeling ready to take on the day's tasks is a sign of a balanced and sattvic state.

Brahma muhurtham-

In order to experience this heightened awareness most yoga schools stress yoga meditation during brahma muhurtham. To be precise it starts 1 hour 36 minutes prior to sunrise and lasts for 48 minutes. Brahma Muhurta has certain power to change your life and that too for the better. It holds great importance to people and practitioners for the spiritual purity it holds and how it has the power to put people at ease because of the calm, serene surroundings. It lies at the last quarter of the night when the flowers in nature are blooming, birds are chirping and also our circadian rhythm in the body reaches its peak of alertness. The vibrations during this time are considered highly pure and are great for meditation, yoga or any spiritual activity. Additionally, for students, during the early hours of Brahma Muhurta the mind is relatively undisturbed which allows for concentration, mental clarity and an increased ability to retain knowledge. The absence of distractions allows individuals to dig deeper into their spiritual practices, self-reflection or do any activity requiring deep concentration.

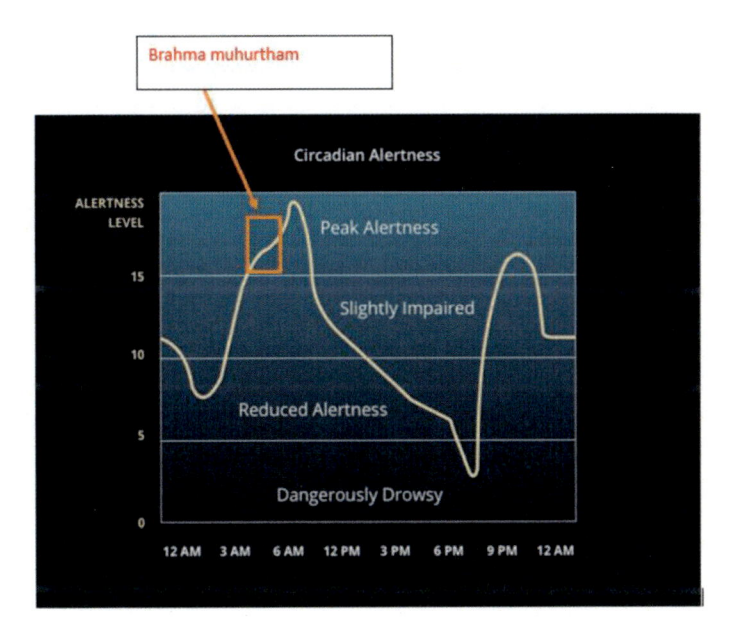

If you look into the graph above based on our body's circadian rhythm (rhythm that runs within our body every 24 hours based on sleep wake cycle), the boxed area is where our alertness reaches the peak, and this coincides with the time of brahma muhurtham. Unfortunately, those who are tamasic or rajasic in nature tend to sleep during this time. Sattvics on the other hand always historically have emphasized on this time being very auspicious and we have scientific evidence today where the peak of alertness reaches 15 and above only during this time in the 24 hour period. Once it reaches the peak it immediately dips down indicating that we need to capture our attention and alertness before it reaches the peak. Hence the time and duration of brahma muhurtham are very specific as mentioned earlier.

5-Smruti (memory)-

Past experiences can leave imprints or samskaras in our minds or chitta. These imprints can influence our perception and response to certain stimuli. For example, if you left your keys inside the car once, you may naturally look for them there again in a similar situation. This reliance on past experiences can sometimes lead to humorous moments, where recalling a funny scene from the past can make us smile or laugh uncontrollably. This highlights how our minds carry a vast collection of samskaras from countless lifetimes, shaping our perceptions and responses to the world around us.

According to Patanjali's teachings, there are two types of memory:

Real memory and Imagined memory.

Real memory refers to factual information that we have experienced and witnessed in our lives. These are events and experiences that we can recall with clarity because they have occurred and left an imprint on our minds. Real memory helps us navigate and make sense of the world around us, allowing us to draw upon past knowledge and experiences to guide our present actions.

On the other hand, imagined memory arises from our dreams and is considered unreal. These memories are products of our subconscious mind and may contain elements that are fantastical or disconnected from our actual experiences.

Memory, or smriti, can indeed be beneficial when it allows us to recall and implement important information from our past into our daily practices. For example, if you remember the technique of Brahmari pranayama, you can incorporate it into your daily routine for its calming and grounding effects.

However, it's crucial to recognize that memory can also have negative implications, especially when it comes to recollecting past traumatic experiences. In cases where traumatic memories are repeatedly and involuntarily recalled, it can result in psychological illnesses such as obsessive-compulsive disorder (OCD) or Post-Traumatic Stress Disorder (PTSD).

In conclusion, Patanjali's teachings regarding the five vrittis or fluctuations of the mind: pramana (correct perception), viparyaya (misunderstanding), vikalpa (imagination), smriti (memory), and nidra (sleep). According to Patanjali, these vrittis can have both detrimental (klesha) and beneficial (aklishta) effects on our yoga practices. Even in the case of Nidra, or sleep, which is considered beneficial for our overall well-being and plays a crucial role in our physical and mental restoration. However, excessive sleep or an imbalanced sleep pattern can make an individual tamasic.

Viparyaya, or misunderstanding, can indeed lead to unexpected outcomes that turn out to be beneficial in the long run. Most used example- At the time of your breakup in your past, you may have believed that your ex-boyfriend would have been the ideal life partner. However, as time passed, you witnessed him causing you and your relationship with significant distress. This revelation opened your eyes to the potential challenges and difficulties that you may have faced had you remained together. So, your initial misunderstanding or viparyaya about your ex-boyfriend's suitability as a life partner turned out to be a blessing in disguise after years of break-up. Often times we thank our lucky stars for clarifying the Viparyaya.

What is the role of vairagya (detachment)? (This is explained again in chapter 7).

The ultimate aim of yoga is to transcend the fluctuations of the mind, including the five basic vrittis, and achieve chitta vritti nirodha, or the cessation of the mind's fluctuations. This state of stillness and clarity allows us to connect with our true selves and experience the profound realization of our inner nature.

To embark on this transformative journey, a true yogi seeks moksha, liberation from the cycle of suffering and the limitations of the ego. One of the key practices on this path is **vairagya,** which can be understood as a desireless or controlled mind. Vairagya involves cultivating a state of detachment from external desires and attachments, recognizing their impermanence and limitations. In the higher state of vairagya, all worldly pleasures and pursuits seem trivial and insignificant compared to the pursuit of spiritual growth and self-realization.

An ignorant person sees the world through the lens of the vrittis, or fluctuations of the mind. These vrittis, which include emotions, judgments, and criticisms, act as a distorted mirror, shaping their perception and understanding of reality. On the other hand, an enlightened person consciously chooses to see the world through their inner self, transcending the limitations of the vrittis. By cultivating vairagya, or detachment, they develop the ability to observe their emotions, judgments, and criticisms without being consumed or controlled by them.

What is the role of Bhoga and Apavarga?

It's fascinating to highlight the dual nature of the mind here as the mind can be used as an instrument for experiencing both the outer world, or **bhoga**, and the inner world, or **apavarga**. The mind serves as a bridge between these two realms, allowing us to engage with the external world and also embark on the path of inner liberation.

In its role as an instrument for experiencing the outer world or **Bhoga**, the mind enables us to engage with our surroundings, form perceptions, and interact with the diverse aspects of life. It allows us to indulge in sensory pleasures, pursue worldly ambitions, and navigate the complexities of our daily existence. Simultaneously, the mind also holds the potential for inner liberation or **apavarga**. Through practices such as meditation, self-inquiry, detachment and mindfulness, we can harness the power of the mind to explore our inner realms, transcend the limitations of the ego, and realize our true nature.

However, among almost all sufferers today, the mind has become their worst enemy. When it is caught up in the grip of negative thoughts, attachments, judgments, or desires, it can lead us down a path of suffering and discontentment. We may become entangled in the illusion that external possessions, achievements, or circumstances will bring lasting fulfillment, only to realize their inherent impermanence and unsatisfactoriness. It is during moments of suffering and disillusionment that we may awaken to the truth that sarvam dukham, or everything is unfulfilling. This realization must not be viewed with pessimism but can serve as a catalyst for inner growth and the recognition that true fulfillment lies beyond the transitory nature of worldly experiences.

Chapter 5

Ignorance is the bedrock of all suffering

Step 14- Ignorant person is far more dangerous than an innocent person.

What is the difference between an innocent and an ignorant person?

Innocence indeed holds a purity that is often reflected in the behavior of children and newborns. They exist in a state where societal rules and the complexities of the world are foreign concepts. They simply are embracing their true nature without judgment or self-consciousness. It is important to recognize that this state of innocence is not by choice rather they are simply not in control of their actions or circumstances.

As a baby, one lacks the knowledge of how to control bodily functions or regulate emotions. Every aspect of their lives, from what they wear to where they go and what they eat, is determined by others. They are entirely dependent on the mercy and care of their caregivers. It would be unfair to label them as "stupid" for their lack of control or understanding.

On the other hand, ignorance, seen particularly in adults who have become disconnected from their true essence. The ego indeed operates under the misconception that the seer, or the true self, and the instruments or external aspects of our being are one and the same. An ignorant person, driven by their ego-based beliefs and limited understanding, can be far more dangerous than an innocent individual.

Ignorance, in this context, refers to a lack of awareness or understanding of oneself and the world around them. It is the result of being caught up in the illusions and conditioning of the ego, which blinds us from seeing the deeper truths of life. An ignorant person may unintentionally cause harm, not only to themselves but also to those around them, including loved ones, friends, and even their own children.

The consequences of ignorance can manifest in various ways. It may lead to destructive behaviors, strained relationships, many illnesses along with a general sense of dissatisfaction and confusion. Many such individuals find themselves seeking answers in the office of a psychologist or by the astrologer or tarot card dealer, questioning Why ME?

In other words, it is important to note that this state of ignorance, though not a deliberate choice but is rather a product of mental conditioning and limited awareness. There are 3 types of ignorant people.

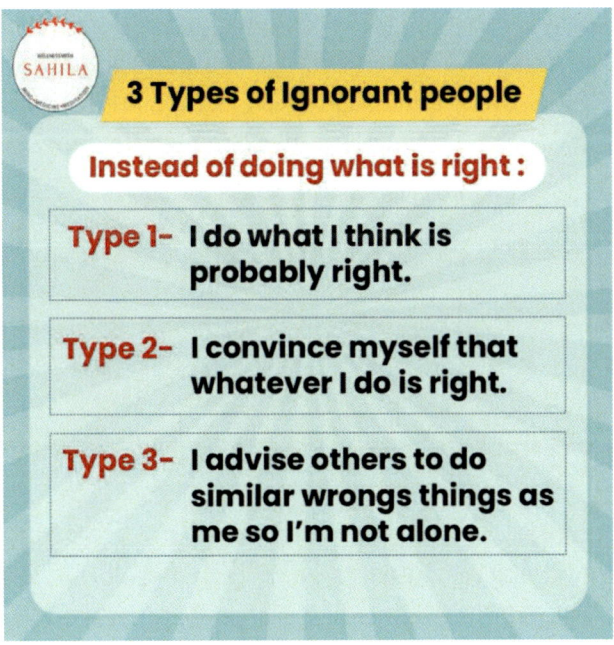

3 Types of Ignorant people

Instead of doing what is right :

Type 1- I do what I think is probably right.

Type 2- I convince myself that whatever I do is right.

Type 3- I advise others to do similar wrongs things as me so I'm not alone.

Type 1 ignorant person-
Instead of doing what is right I do what I think is probably right. Individuals tend to prioritize their own subjective beliefs and perspectives over what is objectively right or beneficial. This can be seen in the example of people who engage in excessive marathon running. While it may not align with medical recommendations or ancient wisdom, they continue to engage in this activity, sometimes participating in multiple marathons per year.

From a medical standpoint, it is not advised to prescribe marathon running as a solution for obesity or illness. The ancient teachings of Yoga or Patanjali also do not specifically advocate for running specific distances to attain ultimate strength or moksha. Engaging in excessive marathon running can be detrimental to one's overall wellness. It puts excessive strain on the knees, which can lead to early wear and tear. Why would someone choose to subject themselves to this unnecessary harm?

One reason is the addiction to the high of endorphins. When they reach the finish line or achieve their running goals, they experience an incredible rush of endorphins that keeps them craving for more. This addiction to the high becomes a driving force, sometimes overshadowing the consideration of potential harm. Like nicotine addiction of 20th century, running a marathon has become a new addiction of the 21st century.

Many of these long-term marathon runners, particularly the overweight, end up in doctors' office with torn tendons, fragmented ligaments and osteoarthritis of the knee. Short term they subject themselves to dehydration, kidney stones, rhabdomyolysis and many such ailments.

Type 2 Ignorant Person-
Instead of doing what is right I convince myself that whatever I do is right. For example- achieving a promotion at work. To achieve

this goal, most people today work until the early hours of the morning, skip meals, and miss important personal events each amounts to an overwhelming amount of stress. The belief that these achievements are necessary for our happiness is a narrative we have created for ourselves. No one dictates that these external markers of success are required for a fulfilling life. This belief is something we have ingrained within ourselves or probably derived from the herd mentality of success.

Another common example-obsession with having a six-pack is prevalent among most men today. While some individuals may naturally have a lean physique that easily reveals their abdominal muscles through exercise, others may struggle despite years of workout in the gym. Comparing ourselves to others and striving for an unrealistic ideal can lead to frustration, self-doubt, and a negative body image.

Excessive consumption of certain foods, especially meat & alcohol, injecting steroids and street drugs in large quantities, can lead to dilated cardiomyopathy, which is a common heart condition in young individuals. This condition can increase the risk of heart attacks, particularly in men under the age of 50. Dilated cardiomyopathy primarily affects young hearts and is now recognized as the leading cause of sudden death among young athletes. It is important to be aware that this condition is not typically seen in older individuals but rather in the age group of 20 to 50 years. While motivational videos showcasing extreme diets and intense workout routines may be captivating, it is essential to approach them with caution and critical thinking.

Type 3 Ignorant person-
Instead of doing what is right I also advise others to do similar wrong things like me so I'm not alone. For example- a doctor recommends that everyone should consume milk without fully understanding the potential implications. It is important for

professionals, especially those in the medical field, to base their recommendations on well-informed and evidence-based practices. Simply relying on personal beliefs or societal norms without conducting thorough research can lead to misguided advice.

In the specific case of milk consumption, it is crucial to consider factors such as the source of the milk and any potential hormones or additives that may be present. Understanding the impact of these factors on one's health is essential for making informed decisions. (To learn more on how milk and milk products can cause cancer please read my book- The Why Behind Cancer published in 2023).

Doctors and healthcare professionals have a responsibility to continually educate themselves and stay updated on the latest research and developments in their field. Let us recognize that our patients place their trust in us, seeking guidance and expertise in matters of health and well-being. It is our duty to approach our profession with diligence, integrity, and a commitment to providing accurate and well-informed guidance.

Step 15- Remove the obstacles in your path or kleshas.

There are indeed five kleshas, or obstacles, in the path of wisdom. These kleshas are mental activities that can manifest in various forms such as thoughts, emotions, sensations, information, and memories. These obstacles can hinder our progress on the path of acquiring true knowledge and prevent us from experiencing true peace and liberation. It is important to understand and recognize these kleshas in order to overcome them.

1-Avidya

Vidya means knowledge and hence avidya is the opposite of vidya, which means ignorance or lack of knowledge. It is important to understand that avidya does not imply that a person is inherently foolish or dumb. Rather, it signifies areas in which each of us lacks awareness or understanding. We all have strengths and weaknesses, and avidya manifests differently in various aspects of our lives. For example, someone may excel in sports but struggle with personal hygiene. Another person might be diligent in maintaining personal hygiene but find it challenging to navigate relationships. And yet another individual may possess strong relationship skills but struggle with addiction, such as drinking.

Avidya serves as the foundation for the other four kleshas or obstacles—asmita (ego), raga (attachment), dvesha (aversion), and abhinivesha (fear of death). By recognizing our areas of avidya, we can gain insight into our strengths and vices and work towards improvement. It is crucial to note that avidya is not limited to individuals but extends to society as a whole. For example- Why do wars occur even today despite knowing that it kills millions of innocent people and cause immense suffering to humanity? Ignorance is a prevalent factor that distorts our perception of the outside world, limiting our understanding and causing us to view things through a narrow lens.

2-Raaga

An important aspect of Raaga is attachment or liking. While it is natural for us to have preferences and desires, it is crucial to recognize the potential consequences when our attachments begin to affect others in a negative way. For example- when I pass by a Ben & Jerry's ice cream shop, I get a strong desire to indulge in my favorite sundae with nuts and strawberries. This type of attachment, rooted in pleasant memories and personal enjoyment, may seem harmless as it primarily affects my own health and well-being.

However, when attachment extends beyond personal preferences and begins to infringe upon the rights and peace of mind of others, it becomes problematic. For example- when a young boy becomes infatuated with a stranger girl and engages in unwanted advances or stalking, then this is a clear example of how raaga can lead to harassment and disturbance. Extreme cases of above can indeed result in serious offenses such as rape, abuse, and bullying. These actions not only harm others but also lead to mental disturbances for all parties involved. It is crucial to recognize such potential harm caused by unchecked or extreme attachments and take responsibility for our actions and their impact on others.

In the path of yoga, the goal is to cultivate detachment and overcome the influence of raaga. This does not mean suppressing our desires or denying our preferences, but rather developing a sense of balance and understanding that respects the autonomy and well-being of others.

3-Dvesha

While love and attachment (raaga) can have positive effects at times, aversion and hatred (dvesha) can be powerful and deeply destructive. Throughout history, we have witnessed instances of dvesha leading to conflicts and misunderstandings among different relationships and when this hatred is projected over a society, it can lead to even wars. Hatred against specific subgroups, such as religious, racial, or ethnic groups, has fueled discrimination, violence, and immense suffering.

The example of Hitler's hatred towards Jews is a chilling reminder of the extreme consequences that dvesha can have. Stemming from personal experiences or distorted beliefs, this deep-seated aversion led to the persecution and genocide of millions of innocent individuals. It is important to recognize that dvesha not only harms those who become targets of hatred but also negatively impacts the individuals harboring these feelings. Dvesha or hatred whether it's directed to someone else or to one's own self as in self-pity is a potent signal to suppress our own immune system often becoming targets of autoimmune illnesses and cancer.

4-Asmita

Asmita or extreme sense of self. It is true that in Western society, there is a strong emphasis on individual identity and the pursuit of personal desires and goals. This can manifest in various ways, from identifying with specific ideologies or labels to embracing self-centeredness and narcissism. For example, a narcissist is infatuated with his own mind and body, or a terrorist driven by extreme Asmita, has deep rooted beliefs about religion or ethnicity. Often dangerous consequences can arise from unchecked self-centeredness. These distorted perspectives can lead individuals down destructive paths, harming themselves and others in the process.

Attempting to reason with someone who holds extreme beliefs rooted in asmita can be incredibly challenging. Their rigid mindset and persuasive tactics may even sway others to adopt their harmful ideologies. It is crucial to approach such situations with caution and seek peaceful resolutions through open dialogue, empathy, and understanding whenever possible.

5-Abhinivesha

It is the fear of death and clinging to life. It is natural for us to desire a peaceful and painless transition from this life to the next, free from suffering and discomfort. However, the reality is that many deaths are accompanied by illness, pain, and various hardships. Sadly, not everyone is fortunate enough to have a peaceful passing. Many individuals experience diseases, physical pain, and disabilities that not only affect themselves but also impact their loved ones. The financial burden of medical treatments, conflicts within families over caregiving responsibilities, and even instances of abandonment or unclaimed bodies on the streets all reflect the challenging circumstances that can surround death.

It is disheartening to consider the fate of unclaimed bodies, which may end up being used for scientific experiments or dissected for educational purposes. These scenarios highlight the harsh realities that some individuals face even in death. Death is an inevitable part of life, and by cultivating acceptance and understanding, we can navigate this profound transition with grace and dignity.

The removal of 5 KLESHAS OR OBSTACLES leads to the dissolution of the distinction between the seer (Drashta) and the seen (Drishti), ultimately leading to liberation. This liberation is often referred to as nirvana, moksha, mukthi, or kaivalya. For a dedicated meditator, this journey can be challenging. The practice of maintaining a continuous state of awareness and allowing wisdom to flow in every moment is indeed a formidable task. It requires a deep commitment and dedication towards the path of yoga, including the practice of the eight limbs and the process of Shuddhi or cleansing.

Through the purification of the mind, one can cultivate a sattvic state—a state free from desires and delusions. By practicing the eight limbs of yoga, (Yamas, Niyamas, Asanas, Pranayama, Dhyana, Dharana, Pratyahara & Samadhi) individuals can gradually detach from the illusions of the external world and attain a state of inner clarity and wisdom.

It is important to recognize that suffering arises not solely from external circumstances such as jathi (birth), ayur (life), or bhoga (experience), but also from our identification with the seer (Drashta), the one who experiences. The wise person understands this and seeks liberation by transcending the limitations of the ego. The journey towards liberation involves a deepening of gnana (knowledge), viveka (discernment), and buddhi (intellect). By cultivating these qualities, one can navigate the cycle of birth and death with awareness and understanding.

At the time of death, if the mind remains fixed in wisdom and the flow of consciousness continues, one can gain insight into their liberation or the nature of their next birth. This is the culmination of the pursuit of liberation, the ultimate goal of the spiritual journey.

Step 16- Every illness originates from the mind.

There are 6 types of thought processes-

A true meditator possesses a deep understanding of their future, allowing their thoughts and desires to manifest into actions. In contrast, an ordinary person who lacks knowledge of meditation may struggle to comprehend their future. As a result, they often face negative consequences from their actions. For example, they may embark on a trip that harms their health or well-being, choose a career path that hinders their professional growth, or select a life partner that leads to disastrous outcomes or divorce.

1-Thoughts originated out of necessity- They are considered neither bad nor good. For example, when our groceries run out, we think of going to the grocery store to fulfill our need for food. Similarly, we are thinking about paying the mortgage to maintain our residence. These thoughts are rooted in our daily necessities, mostly mundane boring types of thought and yet one needs to think about them almost on a daily basis. We think about brushing our teeth and refueling our cars almost every day out of necessity.

2-Thoughts that arise from our habits- For example, we think about using the bathroom in the morning because it's a habitual routine. Similarly, someone who has developed an alcohol addiction may think about alcohol after dinner due to their habit. Good habits are formed from positive thoughts, while bad habits arise from negative thoughts. Even dieting can be transformed into a beneficial habit rather than a challenging task. For instance, having lunch at a specific time, like 1 pm, can be a healthy habit. However, if someone trains their mind to have lunch later, such as 3 pm, and dinner at a much later time like 9 pm, they may unknowingly invite obesity and obesity related health issues.

3-Thoughts that arise from specific circumstances -ex- for instance, if my child seems unwell, I think about taking her to the doctor. Similarly, when my brother is getting married in India, I consider traveling there. These thoughts emerge based on the circumstances at hand and become significant in those moments. Likewise, when I visit a temple and witness others receiving Prasad, even if I am not hungry or it is not yet time to eat, I may end up consuming something due to the circumstances. Thoughts and subsequent actions that arise here are both rare, yet situation related.

4- Thoughts originated from other people's thoughts- our thoughts can also be influenced by the thoughts of others. For example, if a neighbor shares negative information about a new neighbor, it can shape our perception and thoughts about that individual. Conversely, if the same neighbor speaks positively about the new neighbor, it can generate good thoughts and curiosity to meet them. Our thoughts can be influenced by the company we keep and the information we absorb. For instance, regularly listening to your guru's videos and podcasts can impact our thoughts and actions. We can also call them borrowed thoughts or shared ideas. Therefore, it is important to surround ourselves with like-minded individuals who can guide our thoughts in a positive direction. This explains why friends who smoke often influence others to smoke, and the same goes with people who consume excessive alcohol.

Let's see another familiar example- While walking in the mall, you may come across a tempting picture of a McDonald's burger on a poster. Even though it's not lunchtime and it's not your usual habit to eat fast food, the shopkeeper knows that such visuals can influence your thoughts to benefit their business. However, acting upon thoughts influenced by others often leads to regret. After indulging in that burger and fries, you may regret falling for the poster's appeal. Many such people end up blaming the fast-food franchises because they have no control over their thoughts and can easily succumb to the thoughts of others.

 People who easily get influenced tend to blame others for their misfortunes. This is how gossip stories develop within communities or friend groups. Individuals who act consciously and in alignment with their own beliefs are less likely to blame others for their hardships. Only those who unconsciously follow others or get influenced by unwanted ideas end up blaming others for unfavorable outcomes. Gossip stories often trace back to someone or something that started as a mere possibility and later transformed into a definite idea. So let only the thoughts that matter to you linger within you. All other thoughts that seem useless or harmful to you, try to keep them away from you. This can be done by practicing Antar Mouna while meditation.

5-Thoughts that are genetic or karmic in nature-Indeed, our upbringing and the influences of our parents can shape our inclinations and interests. For example- If my father practices and believes in yoga, I may have a genetic predisposition towards it. Similarly, if my mother is an actress, I may feel inclined to pursue a similar path. The same can apply to professions like business, where children often follow in their father's footsteps. Additionally, if we witness our father drinking alcohol daily, it can deeply influence our thoughts and lead to the development of a drinking habit as a means of escaping certain situations. Sometimes, we may feel a sense of obligation or natural inclination to fulfill the dreams or projects left unfinished by our ancestors, such as constructing a temple or completing a school or hospital. While no one explicitly tells us to do so, these inclinations can arise naturally within us.

I remember my grandmother's deep interest in healing people. Even at the young age of 5, I often witnessed her conducting prayers and meditating for those who sought her help. Despite not knowing languages like Telugu, which a couple from a neighboring village spoke, she amazed me during one particular meditation session. She started speaking fluently in Telugu and asked questions that only that couple would know. Witnessing this left me in awe. Looking back, I realize that somewhere within me, those genes are hidden. Helping people heal brings me immense satisfaction, and I find it effortless to communicate in five different languages, both spoken and written. Even though I could have pursued a lucrative career as a physician, my natural inclination towards healing has grown over time. Seeing someone overcome their problems and heal brings me the greatest joy and I live for that passion every single day. These are thoughts and ideas that originated from my grandmother and even today I thank her for that.

6- Thoughts originated from the divine- Rare and powerful thoughts can originate directly from the divine. Only those who engage in intense meditation practices can develop such intuitions and receive thoughts from a higher source. I have shared many such intuitions I received from the divine even in my previous books as well. Here is another such example- During a period of struggle with depression 10 years ago, I found myself contemplating divorcing my husband due to frequent arguments and mood swings, most of which I realize now that I were to be blamed. However, the divine intervened then and conveyed a different message to me. HE assured me that this was a temporary setback in my marriage and emphasized the importance of our partnership in achieving my future dreams. The divine instructed me to trust HIS guidance and promised me a wonderful life with my partner in future if I followed HIS instructions.

Today my husband supports all my programs in addition to managing the marketing and making important financial decisions for wellness with sahila. I blindly trusted the divine's thoughts and followed HIS decisions, which has transformed my life. When I made the decision to leave my six-figure salary 5 years ago and shared my vision for the future, expressing my desire to build a wellness organization, he never judged my intentions. Instead, he believed in me and in my intentions and hence now I'm able to live a fulfilling life with my partner, experiencing a true partnership in every aspect - emotional, spiritual and purpose-oriented.

Whenever a thought arises, it is important to reflect deeply and consider if it aligns with these six factors. By infusing consciousness into our thoughts, we can gain clarity. Once we have developed consciousness within our thoughts, the next step is to determine if they should be translated into action. Remember, we are shaped by our thoughts. How we think influences how we feel, and how we feel influences our actions. Ultimately, our actions determine the outcomes and future of our lives.

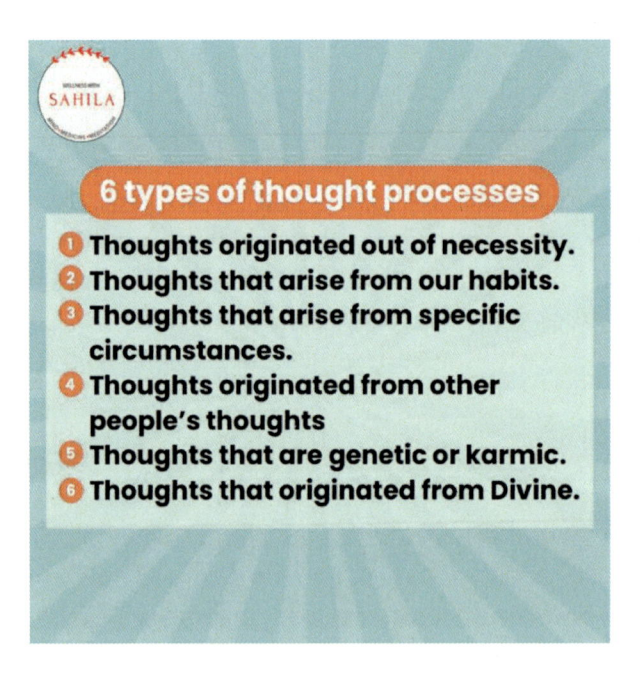

6 types of thought processes

1. Thoughts originated out of necessity.
2. Thoughts that arise from our habits.
3. Thoughts that arise from specific circumstances.
4. Thoughts originated from other people's thoughts
5. Thoughts that are genetic or karmic.
6. Thoughts that originated from Divine.

Chapter 6

What is Suffering or Dukha?

Step 17-Suffering is the state of undergoing constant pain or distress.

When we get afflicted by negative thoughts or vitarkas they harass our minds and lead to suffering. A person who practices yamas and niyamas becomes a maha siddhi or maha yogi and becomes free from suffering. Yoga pathway to suffering is very complex and has many contributors. Understanding this pathway and comprehending how each factor can add to your suffering (or bliss in case of siddhis and Jnanis) is the complete essence of this book. If you have read the book until now paying attention to each step alongside this pathway will become reasonable to follow. (In this chapter I will further elaborate on Gunas, Buddhi, Ahankara & Samakaras and its role on our life).

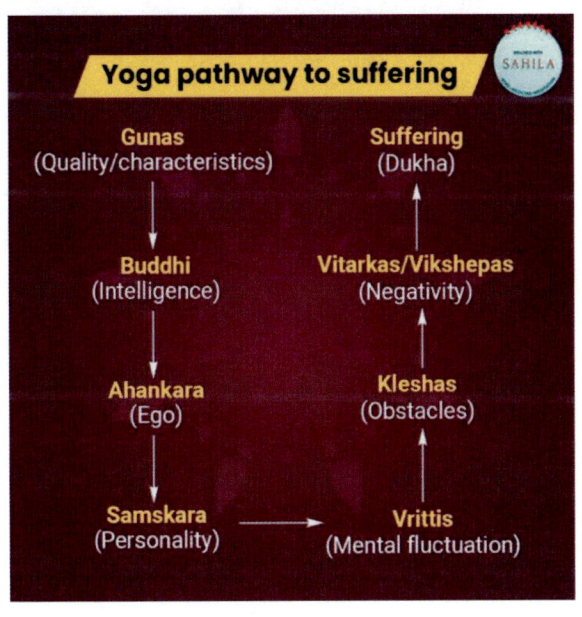

Yoga pathway to suffering

Gunas (Quality/characteristics) → Buddhi (Intelligence) → Ahankara (Ego) → Samskara (Personality) → Vrittis (Mental fluctuation) → Kleshas (Obstacles) → Vitarkas/Vikshepas (Negativity) → Suffering (Dukha)

Gunas- (Quality/Characteristics)

As we embark on the new cycle of birth, we carry our chitta or atma, along with its previous imprints or memories. It is important to note that only certain imprints bear fruit in our present lives. For instance, if you were skilled in archery in a previous birth but are not exposed to it in this life, that skill will not manifest. On the other hand, if you were a dancer in your previous birth, it is possible that you will excel in dance in this life, even without formal training. This natural talent can be attributed to the chitta or previous memory. The 3 fundamental gunas are Sattva, Rajas & Tamas. All beings and things (food or place for example) are a combination of these three gunas, with one or more gunas being dominant at any given time. The goal is to cultivate sattva guna and reduce the influence of rajas and tamas. By doing so, individuals can strive for spiritual growth, self-realization, and liberation from the cycle of birth and death.

Some individuals naturally develop the sattva guna without any external guidance or advice. This can be attributed to their chitta, or the imprints and memories carried from past lives. Just as a dancer may excel in dance without formal training due to their previous imprint, individuals who naturally exhibit qualities of wisdom, compassion, and peacefulness may have cultivated these traits in their previous lives. Their chitta carries the imprints of these qualities, allowing them to naturally embody and express them in their present life.

Buddhi- Intelligence

Buddhi refers to the intellect or the faculty of discernment. It is considered as the higher aspect of the mind, responsible for reasoning, discrimination, and decision-making. It helps individuals differentiate between right and wrong, truth and falsehood, and guides them towards spiritual growth and self-realization. By utilizing our buddhi we can understand how to avoid pancha vrittis and kleshas. (explained in chapter 4).

When kids are born with Autism and ADHD (attention deficit hyperactivity disorder) or Learning disability or Cerebral palsy their Buddhi is compromised from birth and hence their decision-making abilities are poor. Such kids will need parental support even as adults for most important life decisions. The majority of us who have been blessed with normal amount of buddhi yet continue to suffer because we end up making wrong decisions as adults and this book can act as a guide to overcome such sufferings states.

Ego-Ahankara

Ego, in psychological terms, refers to the sense of self or the individual's identity. It is the part of the mind that creates a sense of separateness and individuality. The ego is driven by self-interest, self-preservation, and the need for validation and recognition. It often manifests as attachment to one's beliefs, desires, and personal identity. While ego serves a purpose in navigating the physical world, it can also lead to self-centeredness, pride, and a distorted perception of reality. Balancing and transcending the ego through the development of **buddhi** and **sattva** (explained above) is often seen as a path towards self-realization.

Superego- Sigmund Freud a popular Austrian neurologist did

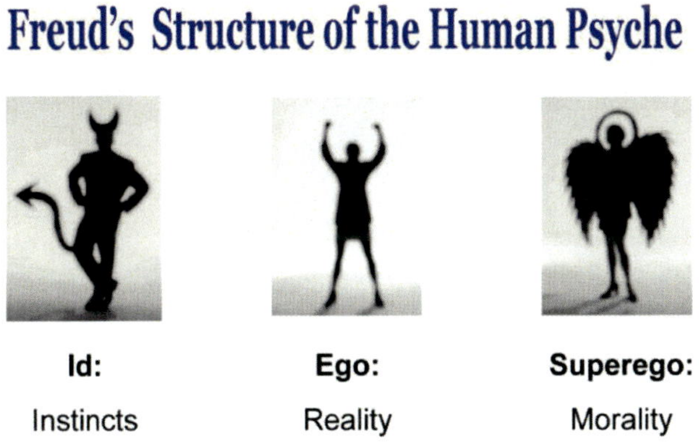

Freud's Structure of the Human Psyche

Id:	Ego:	Superego:
Instincts	Reality	Morality

amazing work on psychoanalysis and his theory comprised of 3 most important concepts which is ID, EGO & SUPEREGO.

The **id** is responsible for impulses and natural urges (and unconscious) part of our psyche that responds directly and immediately to basic urges, needs, and desires. The personality of the newborn child is all id, and only later does it develop an ego and super-ego. The id operates on the **pleasure principle. Example- 3-year-old boy instantly pushes his baby sister for taking his toy away.**

The **ego** is the only part of the conscious personality. It's what the person is aware of when they think about themselves and what they usually try to project toward others. In contrast to the id, the ego follows the **reality principle** as it operates in both the conscious and unconscious mind, and it's oriented towards problem solving. **Example-23-year-old man after being insulted by his boss on poor performance at work, walks into a birthday party smiling.**

The **superego** is the moral component of the psyche, incorporates the values and morals of society, which are learned from one's parents and others. The superego develops during early childhood, operates on the **morality principle** and motivates us to behave in a socially responsible and acceptable manner. Superego is the voice of your consciousness and invokes guilt. **Example-30-year-old woman who murdered her husband repeatedly washes her hands** (obsessive compulsive personality disorder).

Samskaras- Personality development

Samskaras are seen as transformative experiences that shape an individual's character and contribute to their personal growth. The specific samskaras vary depending on the region and community, but some common ones from yogic standpoints include the naming ceremony (Namakarana), the sacred thread ceremony (Upanayana), marriage ceremony (Vivaha), and funeral rites (Antyeshti). Each samskara has its own rituals, prayers, and symbolic actions that are performed to mark the occasion. These samskaras serve multiple purposes. Firstly, they connect individuals to their cultural and religious heritage, ensuring the continuation of traditions and values from one generation to the next. They also provide a sense of belonging and identity within the community. In yoga, samskaras play a pivotal role in establishing the lower 3 chakras (muladhara, swadhisthana & manipura).

For example- Vivaha or marriage ritual that is performed typically at age groups of 20-30 years establishes a firm bond between 2 individuals. It brings together 2 people of different upbringing, different status or education into a union establishing that 1 is a male and another is a female in this union and hence solidifying each of their root chakra or muladhara chakra.

This also allows the couple to engage in sexual union, a well-known component of sacral chakra or swadhisthana. This sexual union then allows the couple to engage in progeny development and their upbringing allowing them to grow as mature individuals while learning to navigate the paths of cyclical changes on birth and death in turn building their karma.

The vivaha or marriage ceremony is usually conducted amidst the elders and extended family members who have personal interests in both the bride and groom. This strengthens the third chakra, the manipura, making space for introducing cousins' uncles and aunts to one another which is what makes the Vivaha such a joyous occasion for everyone in the family. This solidifies our social or Nabhi chakra which is manipura and this concept is key to understanding the importance of maintenance of relationships along with their good and bad.

A person who is very well connected with such samskaras is

unlikely to face blockages in the bottom 3 chakras at the minimum. (to understand more on chakras and how they are connected to our endocrine system and diseases please refer to my book called Chakra Handbook published in 2021).

Vrittis - Mental fluctuations-

It refers to the various patterns and movements of the mind. In the context of yoga and meditation, vrittis are considered disturbances or fluctuations that can disrupt our mental state and hinder our ability to attain inner peace and clarity. The term "vritti" comes from the Sanskrit word "vritti," which means "to whirl" or "to turn." It represents the ever-changing nature of our thoughts, emotions, and perceptions. These fluctuations can manifest as restless thoughts, desires, fears, memories, and other mental activities that arise and pass away within our consciousness.

According to the Yoga Sutras of Patanjali (total of 196 sutras or verses), an ancient text on yoga philosophy, the goal is to cultivate a state of "chitta vritti nirodha," (sutra 1.2) which translates to "the cessation of the fluctuations of the mind." By observing and understanding the vrittis, we can learn to detach from them and cultivate a more focused and tranquil state of mind. Pancha vrittis has been explained in full detailed manner in chapter 4 of this book. (the Human mind).

Kleshas – Obstacles

Kleshas, in the context of yoga are the five afflictions or sources of suffering that cloud the mind and hinder spiritual growth. These afflictions are considered to be the root causes of human suffering and the obstacles to achieving inner peace and enlightenment. The five kleshas are: Avidya, Raaga, Dvesha, Asmita & Abhinivesha. Again, this has been described in length in chapter 5 (Ignorance is the bedrock of suffering.)

Step 18- Negative mind can never give you a positive life.

Vitarkas (mental exploration), Vikshepas (agitation), & Vignanas (contemplation) –

These terms are often used to describe the fluctuations and experiences that occur within the mind during meditation and during the journey of self-discovery. Together they form a cloud of negativity and it's commonly referred to as Antaraya. Indeed, the term "antar" in Sanskrit can be translated as "gap" or "in-between." Vitarkas, vikshepas & vignanas are distractions that create a gap or distance between the true self and the path of spiritual growth. To progress and advance to the next stage in life, it is essential to bridge or shorten this gap by removing the obstacles that hinder our journey. There are 12 main reasons for the cause of such negativity and here we will explore each factor in detail with examples.

Negativity
(Vitarkas Vikshepas Vignanas)
Vyadhi -illness
Styana -idleness
Samsaya- Indecisive
Pramada- carelessness
Alasya-laziness
Avirathi- mental greed
Bhranti Darshana-Delusion
Alabdha Bhumikatva-feeling stuck
Anavasthi tattva- total instability
Dukha- suffering
Daurmanasya- frustration
Angam ejayatva- panic

1-**Vyadhi, or illnesses,** can manifest as physical and mental ailments resulting from an imbalance in the body and mind. In Ayurveda, these imbalances are often attributed to the doshas - Vata, Pitta, and Kapha. Physical pain is a common symptom of these imbalances. Conditions such as back pain, knee pain, headaches, and others can arise when the body's natural equilibrium is disrupted. If left unaddressed, these initial symptoms can lead to more severe complications.

For example, in the case of diabetes, if an individual neglects their blood sugar levels, it can result in the development of wounds, particularly in the feet. Ignoring these wounds can lead to further complications, such as infection, which can eventually reach the bone. In extreme cases, amputation of the foot may be necessary. It is crucial to pay attention to the early signs of illness and take appropriate measures to address them.

2- **Styana or idleness** or a lack of interest in work. Individuals exhibiting this attitude tend to do the bare minimum required to get by, without a genuine desire to excel, learn, or improve. Their primary focus is often on receiving a paycheck rather than actively engaging in personal or professional growth.

This attitude can extend beyond the workplace to other aspects of life, such as homemaking or caregiving. For example, someone with a styana mindset may only do laundry when they have no more clean undergarments left or search for food in the fridge only when they are extremely hungry. This approach leaves them ill-prepared to face challenges, as their body and mind are not adequately primed for optimal performance. To overcome styana, it is important to cultivate a sense of purpose, motivation, and enthusiasm in all areas of life.

3- **Samsaya or indecisiveness,** which refers to doubt or being constantly indecisive about various aspects of life. An example -a man having two wives despite knowing it is illegal and chaotic, yet he struggles to make a choice and continues to suffer as a result.

This indecisiveness can extend to everyday situations as well, such as choosing between a yellow or red saree while shopping. Individuals experiencing samsaya may seek external validation or input from others, like friends or family members, to make decisions. Overcoming samsaya involves developing self-confidence, trust in one's own judgment, and the ability to make decisions without excessive hesitation.

4-Pramada or carelessness or negligence of the facts. It is indeed common to observe adults who are well aware of the effects of alcohol still serving it often times in front of minors. The irony is when they begin expressing concern or disapproval when their teenage children engage in drinking or face the consequences of their actions, such as accidents.

This behavior can be seen as contradictory, as individuals who have previously consumed alcohol may not have considered or cared about its negative effects. However, when it comes to their children, they suddenly advise against drinking, recognizing the potential dangers. It is important to acknowledge that pramada can manifest in various aspects of life, not just in relation to alcohol. It is a reminder that we should strive to be consistent in our actions and decisions, taking into account the consequences and responsibilities associated with them.

5-Alasya or laziness that can contribute to bigger worldwide problems. For example- The combination of factors such as illness, idleness, indecisiveness, and carelessness can lead to weight gain and obesity. It is indeed concerning that obesity has become an epidemic in the United States, with approximately 45% of the population currently classified as obese, and projections indicating that this number may reach 50% by 2030.

Addressing this issue requires a holistic approach that goes beyond external factors such as health insurance, doctors, or hospitals. It necessitates a shift in mindset and the removal of ignorance surrounding healthy lifestyle choices. Without addressing the underlying mental patterns and attitudes that contribute to laziness and unhealthy habits, the problem of alasya and its consequences, including obesity, will continue to persist and grow as projected by statisticians.

6-Avirathi or mental greed or the tendency to constantly compare oneself with others. This mindset often leads to a never-ending cycle of dissatisfaction and wanting what others have. Whether it's desiring a Tesla because your neighbor has one, wanting a new saree because someone else has a new one, or feeling resentful about not receiving a promotion like a colleague did, these comparisons can create mental fluctuations and unwanted consequences.

Some individuals spend their entire lives living in this state of comparison, always seeking validation and happiness through external measures. It is indeed true that such people can be easily identified within a group. Their constant need to compare themselves with others often results in a lack of contentment and a perpetual sense of inadequacy.

7-Bhranti darshana or delusion which refers to mistaken knowledge. This can be seen in situations such as Stockholm Syndrome, where a victim develops positive feelings towards their abuser, or in cases of gaslighting, where emotional abuse causes the victim to question their own sanity.

In Stockholm Syndrome, the victim may be physically or sexually abused, yet they are unable to perceive the situation accurately. From an external perspective, it is evident that the victim is in a harmful and unhealthy situation. However, due to the psychological manipulation and trauma bonding, the victim forms a distorted perception and develops empathy or even affection towards their abuser.

Gaslighting, on the other hand, involves the abuser manipulating the victim's perception of reality and making them doubt their own experiences and memories. The abuser may deny their abusive behavior, twist events, or make the victim feel responsible for the harm inflicted upon them. This emotional abuse leads to a state of confusion and delusion, where the victim struggles to discern what is right or wrong.

8-Alabdha bhumikatva, which refers to the failure to attain stages in life or feeling stuck despite efforts in practices like yoga and meditation. Some individuals may find themselves unable to live in peace or find contentment, leading to a sense of being stuck between two worlds.

It is not uncommon to encounter individuals who express a desire to return to their home country, such as India, while living in a different country like the USA. They may harbor negative feelings towards their current location, citing reasons such as visa issues or job opportunities. However, despite their intention to leave, they often find themselves unable to take the necessary steps to progress and remain in a state of limbo. This inability to move forward and transition to the next stage can be attributed to various factors, including attachment, fear, or a lack of clarity about their goals and aspirations.

The same goes for a toxic relationship, where the couple continue to abuse each other despite their unhappiness. In some cases, they may choose to stay together for the sake of their children, even though it goes against their own desires and well-being. This situation can indeed create a feeling of being stuck, as they are compelled to engage in something that goes against their will. Remaining in a toxic relationship can be emotionally and psychologically draining, leading to a sense of entrapment and unhappiness.

9-Anavasthi tattva, which refers to total instability or the inability to maintain a tranquil state for an extended period of time. Individuals experiencing this instability may find temporary solace during meditation or moments of calm, but as soon as they are faced with challenging situations, they quickly revert back to their previous issues.

For example- a woman who sought consultation regarding her husband's affair and her desire for a divorce. Despite a year of separation, fights, and legal battles, she eventually decided to forgive her husband and they lived together for a few weeks. However, this period of happiness was short-lived, as she would suddenly call with news of another fight or problem with her husband. She would claim that she is a changed person citing her increased meditation practice and spiritual experiences, but a single conflict would throw her back into chaos.

The lack of stability in her life not only affects her but also has a significant impact on her children. They become unwitting participants in the emotional roller coaster ride between their parents, which can be even more challenging than having divorced parents. It is essential for individuals experiencing anavasthi tattva to seek support and guidance to address the underlying issues that contribute to their instability.

Step 19- Types of suffering

(For the sake of simplicity here I have explained the last 3 types of negativities which is Dukha, Daurmanasya & Angam Ejayatva).

Dukha or suffering can be classified further into 3 sub types based on the source of suffering.

1-Adhyatmika: Suffering caused from one's own body and mind: This type of suffering encompasses various physical and mental conditions that individuals may endure. Examples include obesity, depression, diabetes, high BP, pancreatitis, gastritis, insomnia, anxiety etc. These afflictions can cause immense pain, distress, and challenges in daily life. The majority of the suffering seen today (70 percent) in urban settings are arising from this type.

2-Adibautika: Suffering caused by another person or animal: This type of suffering arises from the actions or behaviors of others. It includes instances of abuse, rape, murder, and even the systemic suffering experienced by the poor in a socio-economic structure where wealth is concentrated in the hands of a few. The principle of aparigraha, or non-hoarding, suggests that individuals, even if they are affluent, should keep only what they truly need and generously donate the rest to alleviate the suffering of others. In this case, suffering inflicted upon by other animals like snake bites or lion bites is considered as adibautika. This type of suffering may contribute to 20 percent of the suffering seen today.

3-Adidaivika: Suffering caused by natural calamities: This type of suffering stems from uncontrollable natural events such as earthquakes, tornadoes, famine, pandemics, forest fires, and tsunamis. These disasters can lead to immense loss, destruction, and the displacement of communities, resulting in significant suffering for those affected. This type of suffering may contribute to the last 10 percent seen today and is rarest form of suffering.

It's interesting to note that Adhyatmika and Adibautika types of sufferings can be minimized or controlled to a large extent by adopting changes in our lifestyles as well as reprograming our mind as suggested so far in this book. Adidaivika type is beyond our control. In other words, close to 90 percent of our suffering can be minimized if we pay close attention to the suffering flow chart mentioned in the beginning of this chapter.

4- Daurmanasya- dejection or frustration arising from disturbances in the mind.

This can be observed in situations where individuals experience a shift in their emotional state based on external factors, even though they are aware of the impermanence of those factors.

For example, a poor man who is experiencing distress due to a lack of money may be in pain. However, if the same man suddenly obtains a treasure or wealth, he becomes joyful. Despite knowing that the newfound wealth is not permanent, his state of mind becomes dependent on impermanent things like money or material possessions.

Similarly, let's consider the scenario of a young 10-year-old girl who desires to have a grand birthday party to impress her friends. If, for some reason, a calamity strikes the family and her father loses the financial means to throw the party, the little girl will instantly become sad. She may be aware that the party is a temporary event, lasting only a few hours, but those hours determine whether her mind is in a state of happiness or distress.

These examples highlight the impact of external circumstances on our emotional well-being. They demonstrate how our minds can become attached to fleeting experiences or material possessions, leading to repeated fluctuations in our state of happiness or distress.

5- **Angam Ejayatva- panic attacks**

Panic can be intense and overwhelming experiences that can affect both our physical and mental well-being. When faced with situations that trigger fear or uncertainty, such as receiving life threatening test results or encountering a potential threat like a robber entering our house, it is natural for our bodies to react with heightened physiological responses.

During a panic attack, our limbs may shake and tremble, our heart rate increases, and we may start sweating and even feel like fainting. These physical manifestations are often accompanied by a flood of anxious thoughts and a sense of fear that can consume our minds. Even individuals who have developed a strong sense of inner calm through practices like yoga & meditation can find themselves in a state of panic when faced with immediate danger or distressing situations. It is a human response to prioritize self-preservation and react instinctively to potential threats. While it is important to acknowledge and validate these experiences, it is also beneficial to cultivate tools and coping mechanisms to manage panic and anxiety.

Chapter 7

Steps to overcome suffering

Step 20- Treat the cause not the symptoms.

Following the yamas & niyamas is the best approach to treating the cause of suffering. Yamas and Niyamas are ethical principles and guidelines that form the foundation of yogic philosophy and practice. They also provide a framework for living a balanced, ethical, and meaningful life. To understand what the benefits of those practices are, please take a look at the below posts. There are certain similarities between yamas and niyamas but there are certain differences as well that make them stand apart.

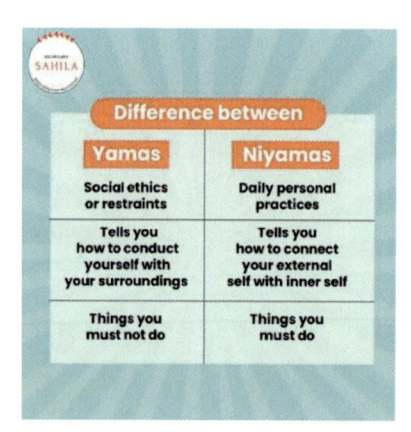

Difference between	
Yamas	**Niyamas**
Social ethics or restraints	Daily personal practices
Tells you how to conduct yourself with your surroundings	Tells you how to connect your external self with inner self
Things you must not do	Things you must do

Similarities between Yamas and niyamas
1. They are moral codes for every human being aspiring to be a yogi
2. They are written in the heirarchy of practice
3. They help unlock your spiritual potential and allow other paths of yoga easy to follow
4. They are absolute rules and applicable to all ages and times
5. They are preliminary steps one must follow before mastering other limbs of raja yoga and makes one attain sidhhi.

Yamas:

Ahimsa (Non-violence): This principle emphasizes non-violence in thought, speech, and action. It involves cultivating compassion, kindness, and harmlessness towards oneself and others.

Satya (Truthfulness): Satya encourages honesty, truthfulness, and integrity in all aspects of life. It involves speaking and living in alignment with our true nature and avoiding falsehood.

Asteya (Non-stealing): Asteya promotes the practice of non-stealing, both in terms of material possessions and intangible aspects such as time, energy, or ideas. It encourages contentment and gratitude for what we have.

Brahmacharya (Moderation): Brahmacharya suggests practicing moderation and channeling our energy towards higher pursuits. It involves cultivating self-control, balance, and mindful use of our physical, mental, and emotional energy.

Aparigraha (Non-possessiveness): Aparigraha encourages non-attachment and non-possessiveness. It involves letting go of excessive desires, greed, and clinging to material possessions, fostering a sense of contentment and detachment.

Advantages of Yamas & niyamas

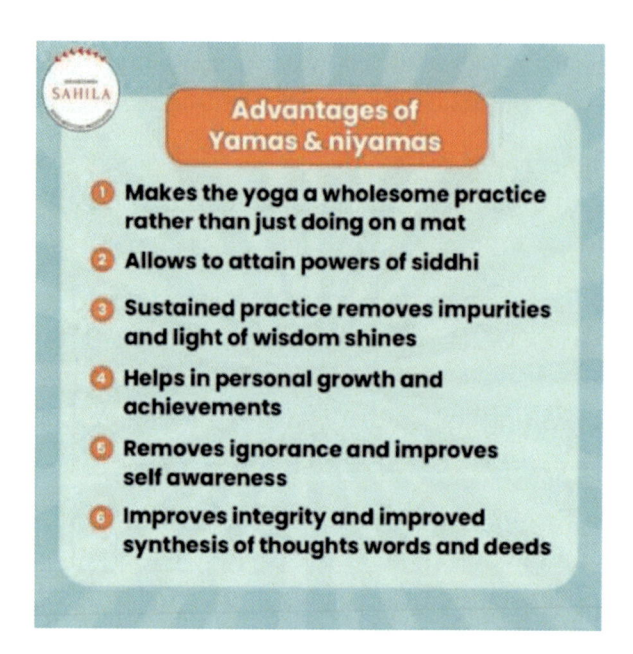

1. Makes the yoga a wholesome practice rather than just doing on a mat
2. Allows to attain powers of siddhi
3. Sustained practice removes impurities and light of wisdom shines
4. Helps in personal growth and achievements
5. Removes ignorance and improves self awareness
6. Improves integrity and improved synthesis of thoughts words and deeds

Niyamas:

Saucha (Purity): Saucha emphasizes cleanliness and purity, both externally and internally. It involves maintaining a clean physical environment, as well as purifying our thoughts, emotions, and intentions.

Santosha (Contentment): Santosha promotes contentment and gratitude for the present moment and what life offers. It involves finding satisfaction and joy in the present rather than constantly seeking external validation or material possessions.

Tapas (Discipline): Tapas refers to the practice of self-discipline, perseverance, and austerity. It involves cultivating inner strength, willpower, and dedication to our spiritual growth and personal development.

Svadhyaya (Self-study): Svadhyaya encourages self-reflection, self-study, and the study of sacred texts. It involves gaining self-awareness, understanding our true nature, and deepening our knowledge and wisdom.

Ishvara Pranidhana (Surrender to a higher power): Ishvara Pranidhana involves surrendering to a higher power or divine will. It involves recognizing that there is a greater force at play and cultivating trust, surrender, and devotion.

In addition to the yamas and niyamas there are certain other factors that help in preventing suffering which are not so widely understood and often ignored. I have classified them into **level 1 practice** which can be incorporated by most and **level 2 practice** which is incorporated only after several months or years of level 1 practice.

For people who are still new to yoga & meditation it's always good to start with level 1 practice which is simpler and easy to follow by almost anyone.

1-Abhyasa-

The principle of continuous practice emphasizes the importance of consistent and dedicated effort in the realm of yoga and

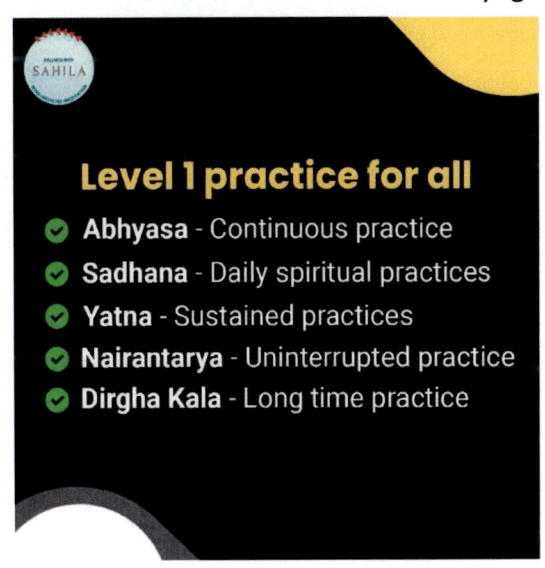

Level 1 practice for all
- **Abhyasa** - Continuous practice
- **Sadhana** - Daily spiritual practices
- **Yatna** - Sustained practices
- **Nairantarya** - Uninterrupted practice
- **Dirgha Kala** - Long time practice

meditation. Regardless of how much theoretical knowledge one possesses, without practical application, it holds little value. Without engaging in regular practice, one remains akin to an ignorant person, lacking the experiential wisdom that comes from direct engagement. Therefore, Abhyasa encourages individuals to commit themselves to consistent practice, without making excuses or taking breaks. The best time to start Abhyasa would be during sunrise (before your morning coffee or breakfast) or sunset (before dinner).

2-Sadhana-

Daily spiritual practices- 6 daily practices are mandated and emphasized to all my students. -Daily yoga & daily meditation, daily morning start the day with a list of things to do or goals for the day, daily spend at least few minutes with nature (walking, gardening, breathing exercises done outdoors, or just having tea in backyard) , daily thank someone or something before going to bed, daily journal your thoughts (so you can speak to yourself clearly and honestly and also see the progress of your thoughts as time passes by), daily eat sattvic food by following 15 sattvic diet rules. (explained in detail in chapter 1). For those who want to understand what is sattvic diet please refer to my booklet on the website- 15 rules of Sattvic diet customized for US lifestyle.

3-Yatna-

The principle of sustained effort emphasizes the importance of consistent practice even in the face of challenges or disruptions. Regardless of external circumstances such as distress, illness, or work deadlines, it is essential to maintain a dedicated and unwavering commitment to one's practice. Just as we do not take breaks from essential activities like eating, sleeping, or attending to our bodily needs, yatna reminds us that our spiritual practices should be integrated seamlessly into our lives. It becomes a natural and non-negotiable part of our daily routine, regardless of the changes or demands that may arise. By embracing yatna, we recognize that our practices are not separate from the ebb and flow of life.

4-Nairantarya-

The principle of uninterrupted practice emphasizes the importance of maintaining focus and concentration during yoga and meditation sessions. It encourages practitioners to avoid distractions such as watching movies, scrolling through social media, or engaging in conversations on phone while engaging in these practices. By adhering to nairantarya, practitioners create an environment conducive to deepening their practice and reaping its benefits. Uninterrupted practice allows for the development of one-pointedness and concentration, enabling individuals to master the techniques and experience greater levels of focus and clarity. (one that is essential to master pratyahara- limb 5 in raja yoga)

5-Dirgha kala-

The principle of long-term practice serves as a reminder that yoga and meditation are not quick fixes or instant gratification endeavors. In a world that often prioritizes immediate results, it is important to approach these practices with patience and a long-term perspective. Unlike taking a pain pill or ordering food through a delivery service, yoga and meditation require consistent and sustained effort over an extended period. It is through dedicated practice, incorporating all the steps mentioned previously, that the true benefits and results become evident. My personal experience with chakra healing and overcoming depression highlights the power of incorporating all of the level 1 practices for a period of 4 years. By committing to these five steps, regardless of the changes and challenges that life presents, I was able to achieve permanent healing and eliminate the need for depression medication.

Words of Swami Vivekananda here has been my foremost motivation in adhering to level 1 practices and here is that famous quote.

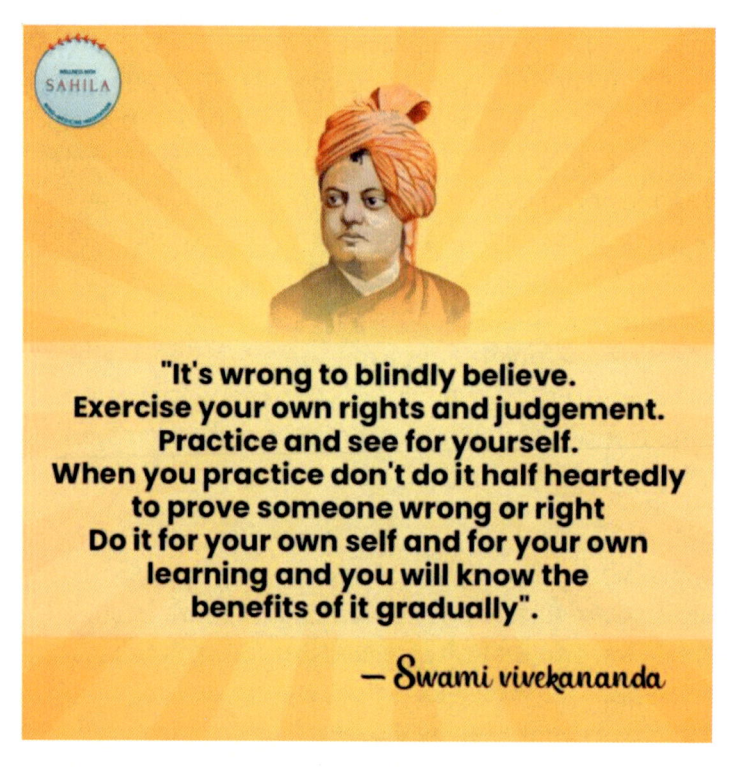

"It's wrong to blindly believe.
Exercise your own rights and judgement.
Practice and see for yourself.
When you practice don't do it half heartedly to prove someone wrong or right
Do it for your own self and for your own learning and you will know the benefits of it gradually".

— Swami vivekananda

If you are able to achieve level 1 practice for a period of months to years, then now you are ready to advance your practice and go to level 2

A dedicated yogi who diligently practices both level 1 and level 2 steps can ultimately attain moksha, which is liberation from suffering. This is comparable to the analogy used by the great sage Vedavyasa, who likened the sattva state to a beautiful garden with fragrant flowers, while rajas and tamas are like weeds and pests that continuously attempt to disrupt the garden's beauty.

To maintain the purity of the garden, we must be like a devoted gardener who consistently tends to it through daily sadhana, which includes the efforts of both levels of practice. The gardener understands that even a single day of neglect can allow the rajasic and tamasic qualities of the mind to overpower the sattvic nature.

If the yogi forgets to practice or takes a day off, their mind can become overwhelmed by negative thoughts (vitarkas) and the sattvic qualities may diminish. Therefore, it is crucial for the yogi to remain dedicated and consistent in their practice, knowing that sustained effort is essential to protect and nurture their inner garden of consciousness.

Level 2 practice to get rid of vrittis
- **Swadhyaya-** Self study
- **Vairagya -** Dispassion or indifference to sense objects
- **Tyaga -** Renunciation of pleasure seeking thoughts
- **Virya -** Quality of effort+energy
- **Pratipaksha bhavana-** break vasanas

1-Swadhyaya-

The principle of self-study emphasizes the importance of introspection and self-reflection to gain a deeper understanding of oneself. It involves examining our thoughts, behaviors, strengths, and weaknesses to cultivate self-awareness and personal growth which includes reading self-awareness books like this.

For example- an individual's inflated ego and inability to acknowledge ones mistakes or apologize may be causing difficulties in relationships. Through swadhyaya, this person can engage in self-study to explore the root causes of their behavior and its impact on their relationships. By delving into their thoughts, beliefs, and patterns of behavior, they can gain insight into the destructive role their ego plays in their interactions. Swadhyaya allows them to recognize their strengths and weaknesses, fostering humility and a willingness to learn from their mistakes. This newfound awareness can lead to personal growth, improved relationships, and a more balanced approach to life.

2-Vairagya-

The principle of dispassion invites us to cultivate a state of indifference towards sense objects and external pleasures. It encourages us to develop a mindset where we are not dependent on the presence or absence of these objects for our well-being.

For example- the attachment to having coffee at a specific time can lead to irritation, headaches, and a disruption in your daily routine if it is not available. However, through the practice of yoga sadhana, you can cultivate vairagya, allowing you to find contentment and peace regardless of whether you have access to coffee or not. By developing indifference towards external pleasures, you free yourself from the fluctuations of desires and attachments. This state of dispassion enables you to find inner stability and joy, independent of external circumstances. Vairagya does not mean denying oneself of enjoyment or pleasure, but rather cultivating a mindset of non-attachment.

3-Tyaga

The practice of renunciation plays a significant role in breaking free from the patterns of desire and attachment that can hinder spiritual growth. It can be challenging for anyone to give up the pursuit of pleasures, as they often bring immediate gratification. However, in the yogic tradition, practitioners often begin by renouncing certain types of food that are detrimental to their health and well-being, even though they may be appealing to the taste buds.

This process typically starts with eliminating sweet and junk foods and gradually transitioning to a sattvic diet. Advanced yogis may choose to consume simple home-cooked meals consisting of raw fruits, nuts, and yogurt. Some may even reduce their intake to just two or one meal a day. As their dependency on food decreases, their requirements diminish, resulting in reduced expenditure of both money and time on food. Furthermore, they may experience the added benefit of improved health. (To learn more about Sattvic diet please refer to my 30 page booklet on my website and this is simplified for US lifestyle).

4-Virya

This refers to the quality of energy and effort. It represents the vigor, vitality, and determination that one brings to their actions and endeavors. Virya is the inner strength and resilience that propels individuals to persevere and overcome obstacles on their path. It is the cultivation of a focused and unwavering commitment to one's goals and aspirations. By harnessing the power of virya, individuals can tap into their inner reserves of energy and drive, allowing them to accomplish great feats and navigate the challenges of life with courage and determination.

For example- A dedicated athlete who trains tirelessly, pushing their physical limits and maintaining a disciplined regimen to achieve peak performance in their sport. An entrepreneur who pours their energy and effort into building a business from scratch, overcoming setbacks and working long hours to make their vision a reality. From my own experience of starting wellness with Sahila from scratch, the sarcasm and mockery I faced in the initial days were overwhelming especially because this is not the traditional route a doctor chooses in USA. When the same few people now appreciate my efforts and sincerity I realize the power of Virya.

5-Pratipaksha Bhavana-Break Vasanas

Pratipaksha Bhavana is a powerful yogic technique that involves cultivating positive and opposing thoughts to counteract negative or harmful ones. It is a practice of consciously redirecting our thoughts and emotions towards positive and constructive perspectives.

.Vasana refers to the deep-rooted impressions or tendencies stored in the subconscious mind. These vasanas influence our thoughts, emotions, and actions, shaping our behaviors and perceptions. They are formed through past experiences and conditioning, and they can continue to influence our present behavior, often leading to repetitive patterns. Vasanas can be positive or negative.

When negative thoughts, emotions, or tendencies arise, Pratipaksha Bhavana encourages us to actively replace them with their positive counterparts. For example, if we experience feelings of anger, we can intentionally cultivate thoughts of compassion and forgiveness. If we find ourselves dwelling on self-doubt, we can intentionally shift our focus towards self-confidence and self-empowerment.

Breaking the negative patterns of habits is an effective way to break the vrittis, or the fluctuations of the mind. For example- When it comes to reducing the consumption of sugar or sweet foods, replacing them with positive habits can be highly beneficial.

When the desire for something sweet arises, one can choose to engage in pranayama, which is a practice of controlling the breath and vital energy. Pranayama helps to calm the mind and redirect the focus away from the craving for sweetness. Additionally, drinking green tea can be a healthy alternative to satisfy the desire for something flavorful. Green tea contains antioxidants and offers various health benefits. By replacing the habit of consuming sugary foods with the habit of drinking green tea, one can gradually reduce the dependency on sweets and cultivate a more balanced and health-conscious lifestyle.

Step 21- Power of Autosuggestion, Humor & Pranayama

Autosuggestion refers to the practice of self-suggestion or self-hypnosis, where individuals use affirmations or positive statements to influence their subconscious mind. By repeatedly affirming positive beliefs or desired outcomes, individuals aim to reprogram their subconscious mind and bring about positive changes in their thoughts, feelings, and behaviors.

Autosuggestion involves consciously and intentionally directing one's thoughts and focusing on specific goals or desired outcomes. For example- my goal in the past 5 years was to become really good with yoga meditation such that I can teach and transform lives. I lived and believed that I could do that every single day even when some days got tough, at times even tough to survive. I tried to never let go of that belief system even during my toughest moments in life. It is based on the belief that the subconscious mind can be influenced and that positive suggestions can help overcome negative thought patterns or limitations. Practice writing those affirmations on a board and stick it on the wall where you face daily.

The practice of autosuggestion often involves creating affirmations or positive statements that reflect the desired outcome or belief. These affirmations are then repeated regularly, either silently or aloud, with the intention of ingraining them into the subconscious mind. So, I repeated these statements in my mind- I'm fully capable of achieving my goals. I'm equipped with knowledge and energy to become a wellness coach. Not only that, I wrote down each goal on a piece of word document and printed it and posted it on my computer screen where I can see every day.

The effectiveness of autosuggestion can vary from person to person, and it is important to approach it with an open mind and consistent practice. It is not a magical solution but can be a valuable tool for self-improvement, personal development, and achieving desired goals.

Humor serves as a means of communication, connecting individuals through shared laughter and amusement. By employing wit, irony, satire, or clever wordplay, humor has the power to entertain, uplift spirits, and provide a temporary respite from life's challenges. Humor can take various forms, such as jokes, puns, anecdotes, or comedic performances, and it often relies on the unexpected or absurd to elicit laughter.

Moreover, humor has been shown to have numerous psychological and physiological benefits. It can reduce stress, improve mood, boost creativity, and strengthen social bonds. In challenging times, humor can provide a much-needed perspective, allowing us to find lightness in the face of adversity.

For example- a person who has a difficult marriage with a wife who curses him daily, often jokes with his colleague "living with my wife has trained me with enough thick skin that my boss words feel like nectar to my ears".

In summary, humor is a wonderful facet of human expression that brings joy, laughter, and connection. It serves as a valuable tool for navigating life's ups and downs, fostering positivity, and creating moments of shared mirth.

Pranayama- Prana is life force, ayama means extention or expansion. So, prana plus ayama is pranayama which means methods to expand life forces. If we don't control our breath, it wanders in the wrong direction. Hence regular practice of pranayama brings the energy back to our breath acting as a check and prevents it being stagnant in odd and uncomfortable places in our body. This is the essence of Pranayama. It's also considered as a bridge to meditation.

How to not let our breath wander in the wrong places and give them a sense of direction?

How to bring a new level of awareness by stopping the distractions of the mind?

In other words- when prana fluctuates then the mind or Chitta also fluctuates and when the prana is still or steady then the Chitta also becomes steady. When asanas are performed correctly then automatically the benefits of pranayama can be felt more easily. While both asanas and pranayama aim for the same thing asana are achieved by physical means by using our body postures while pranayama is achieved by regulation of mind using our breath.

Conscious & unconscious breathing -Normally we breathe 15 times per minute or 21,600 times per day. Hence breathing happens unconsciously most of the time and our breath and our mind wanders. Each pranayama is integrated with a particular system. Every pranayama has a definite role and definite way to be practiced and taught. Most of the pranayama are not taught in most yoga schools in USA because they don't understand the science behind it. Also, pranayamas are subtle exercises which are difficult to explain unlike the physical asanas. It takes a tough and wise guru to teach pranayamas correctly. Some people who have been taught incorrectly lose faith in pranayamas. Hence spend some time here to understand the science behind pranayamas.

Remember in Pranayama we take conscious control over our breath and allow this energy to build our most significant systems like respiratory, immune system, digestive, emotional and intelligent parts of brain function, neurological function. This automatically helps achieve hormonal balance. In this way we are able to release unconscious energy that is trapped in useless things like thinking over the past, worrying about the future, or worrying about kids or finances or job or broken relationships. All that energy is released from those negative unwanted places and brought back to the important functions of the body and revitalizes them.

Breathing slow- The slower the breathing the better for our life. Ancient rishis and yogis observed that animals who breathe faster like birds, insects die faster or have short life span, but animals who breathe slowly lived longer. Because when we slow down our breath work, it slows down consumption of energy and hence it prolongs our lifespan. In the deeper sense it enhances the healthy body by removing blockages within, helps attain tranquility in mind and finally establishes an intimate current with the cosmic nature around us.

3 stages of pranayama- In the initial stages or a beginner in pranayama of pranayama we focus on inhalation and exhalation but in later stages of pranayama we will focus more on kumbhaka or breath retention. This is the most important part of the pranayama and interestingly there is no technical term or medical term for holding the breath. So puraka means inhalation and rechaka means exhalation and there is no terminology for holding in modern medicine because no where in the medical books there is any significance given to this holding so there is no medical term to it. But in pranayama this holding has a name to it called kumbhaka, and not only that it has 3 parts of kumbhaka

Antar kumbhaka, bahir kumbhaka and kevala kumbhaka. Meaning

the beginning, middle and end of holding breath. This is of prime focus in thirumoolar pranayama and that's why this is very essential for unblocking anahata chakra.

. Right is the pingala nadi carrying energy from the muladhara to the agna. It represents the sun or positive or male or yang energy. The left is ida nadi or pathway which carries the moon, cold, female or yin energy to the agna. At any 1 point the flow through 1 nostril predominates over the other. This explains how sometimes we want to be in physical activities and sometimes we want to be in mental activities. Physical activities can be running, walking or climbing stairs. Mental activities can be working in front of the computer, reading a book or watching something on tv or even sleeping is mental activity. Throughout the day we are engaging in both these types of activities alternating with one another. For Some people mental work seems easy. In a 24-hour time allotted in a day, if we divide them into 8 hours, we need to do 8 hours of physical activities, 8 hours of mental activities and 8 hours of sleep. But today we focus predominantly only on mental activities which is our work. Some of us work close to 10 hours or even 12 hours a day. The time allotted for physical activity drops down significantly, because of the physical mental imbalance the sleep gets affected, anxiety, difficulty to fall asleep.

So here in my classes we focus on all 3 aspects physical asanas, mental relaxation using pranayama and deep meditation like yoga nidra or sleep. They can sit in front of the computer for hours and not feel the necessity to get up and walk or exercise. For some physical activity comes easily like the mountain climbers or ocean swimmers or serial marathon runners. They like to engage in some sort of physical activity all the time but ask them to sit still and read a book and they may not be able to do that. Such people who like to engage in more physical activities have more flow in Pingala or right nostril. Ex ADHD or other learning disabilities. People who engage in only mental activities have more flow in ida pathway or left norstril. In reality the ability to think and the ability to act comes from a balance of these 2 pathways. In the modern world we see people getting into motor vehicle accidents or getting arrested for drunk driving or speeding tickets because their ability to act appropriately in a few seconds is compromised. Similarly, for those with very less flow in ida their ability to think correctly is inhibited and they become lazy or unable to make a career for themselves or go into depression easily. In Pranayama we try to achieve a balance of these activities, the ability to act appropriately and ability to think appropriately so pranayama helps prepare that ground for meditation. When that stability is reached then higher meditation like chakra meditation where energy starts flowing in the central path called sushusmna happens naturally.

Certain conditions before commencing pranayama-

Certain pranayama cannot be performed in pregnancy states like kapala bhati.

Regular time of practicing is important to attain higher perfection. So, sunrise or sunset is an ideal time. Remember this is also the best time for any type of yogic practice because our stomachs are usually empty at this time and pitta fire element is low during this time. Certain pranayama like brahmari can also be done before sleep because of its benefit with sleep and relaxation. Avoid showering for atleast an hour after pranayama because body temperatures are low.

Practice in clean quiet rooms. All pranayamas breathe via the nose unless indicated to open the mouth. Ideally pranayamas should be done after asanas and before meditation and that's why the 8-step approach in wholesome yoga is designed in that way.

Sukhasana, Siddhasana or padmasana or sometimes vajrasana is best position for pranayama. Always place head neck & spine erect. If you cannot sit down place yourself on a chair and keep your back straight. Some people feel extremely light after the practice. Sometimes heavy strain can cause light headedness or feeling cold or hot in which case you can stop the pranayama and take guidance from me.

Types of pranayama

Simple pranayamas-
1-anulom vilom (alternate nostril)
2-sheetali
3-sheetkari
4-thyroid pranayama
5-brahmari
6-bhastrika
7-moorcha pranayama (advance)
8-surya bhedana pranayama (simplest of all)
9-chandra bhedana pranayama

Complex pranayamas-
1-ujjayi
2-kapala bhati
3-thirumoolar

To learn the methods of above pranayama, please enroll in my classes.

Bonus Chapter: Addictions

Addiction is a complex condition characterized by compulsive behavior and a strong dependence on a particular substance or activity. It is commonly associated with substances such as smoking, drugs or alcohol, but addiction can also manifest in behaviors like gambling, gaming, or even excessive use of the internet. Addiction is often driven by a combination of biological, psychological, and social factors. It can have severe negative consequences on an individual's physical health, mental well-being, relationships, and overall quality of life. Treatment for addiction typically involves a combination of therapy, support groups, medication, and lifestyle changes to help individuals overcome their dependence and regain control over their lives.

For purpose of simplification, I have picked smoking addiction here and have explained in detail how chakra blockages can lead to such addictive behaviors and eventually Chakra Anonymous discussion groups can be the best and permanent methods for removing such addictions. One can apply the same logic and idea to alcohol addiction or drug addiction, or any other form of addictions seen in the community today.

Modern methods can sometimes fall short in effectively addressing and removing addictions for a few reasons. Firstly, many modern approaches focus solely on treating the symptoms of addiction rather than addressing the underlying causes. This can result in temporary relief but fail to provide long-term solutions. Additionally, some methods may rely heavily on medication without adequately addressing the psychological, emotional, and social aspects of addiction.

Furthermore, modern methods often neglect the holistic nature of addiction, only targeting the physical or behavioral aspects.

WHY QUITTING IS HARD

1. You smoke.
2. Nicotine quickly goes to your brain (as quickly as seven seconds) with each puff.
3. You feel relaxed and good.
4. Your nicotine level falls quickly after smoking a cigarette.
5. You feel a craving for another cigarette (nicotine)
6. You think, "I want a smoke" or feel irritable or restless without it.

← Cycle Starts Over Again

However, addiction is a complex condition that requires a comprehensive approach, considering the individual's mind, body, and spirit.

Lastly, the lack of personalized and individualized treatment can hinder success. Each person's addiction is unique, and a one-size-fits-all approach may not be effective for everyone.

Smoking can indeed have direct and indirect harmful effects on the body.

The direct effects of smoking primarily arise from the chemicals present in tobacco smoke. When smoke is inhaled, it contains numerous toxic substances, including nicotine, tar, carbon monoxide, and many others. These substances can cause damage to various organs and systems in the body.

The tar in cigarette smoke is particularly damaging. It contains numerous carcinogens (cancer-causing agents) that can lead to the development of lung cancer, as well as cancers of the mouth, throat, esophagus, bladder, and other organs. Tar also contributes to the formation of plaque in the arteries, increasing the risk of heart disease and stroke.

In addition, smoking can lead to the development of respiratory conditions such as asthma, chronic obstructive pulmonary disease (COPD), and bronchitis. These conditions can cause symptoms such as coughing, wheezing, shortness of breath, and reduced lung function. Furthermore, smoking increases the risk of cardiovascular diseases, including heart attacks and strokes. The chemicals in tobacco smoke can damage the blood vessels, increase blood pressure, promote the formation of blood clots, and accelerate the development of atherosclerosis (narrowing and hardening of the arteries).

The indirect effects of smoking which we are not taught in med schools or in therapy is that the emotion or attitude with which one is smoking. There are 3 categories of smokers.

Dangerous smokers - The first category of individuals who are at a high risk of developing an addiction to smoking and for most of these people, smoking is their sole source of pleasure in life. These individuals have a limited range of activities and interests, making it particularly challenging for them to quit smoking. It is likely that they have a blockage in their muladhara, or root chakra. In order to effectively address their addiction, it is essential to treat the underlying cause of this blockage. For examples- depressed smokers, smokers with terminal illnesses, smokers who are physically disabled and so on.

Underprivileged smokers- The second category of smokers consists of individuals who view smoking as one of many pleasures in life, similar to alcohol or other drugs. These individuals are often involved in activities such as selling street drugs or participating in mafia gangs or other illegal things. Although they have a moderate chance of developing an addiction, they also have other factors in their lives that provide fulfillment. They are also blocked in muladhara or root chakra and have moderate levels of addiction to smoking. However, if they do not make an effort to quit smoking, it is likely that they will eventually transition into the first category of smokers described earlier.

Privileged smokers- The final category of smokers finds smoking to be a small pleasure, such as indulging in a smoke during a walk or after certain events like experiencing an orgasm or completing a successful work project. Individuals in this category have the lowest likelihood of developing an addiction, and quitting smoking is relatively easier for them compared to the other categories discussed. These people are likely to be blocked in manipura or solar chakra unlike the previous 2 categories who have muladhara blockage (root chakra).

How to identify imbalanced CHAKRAS

- Crown → Brain fog, ego, confusion
- Third eye → Lack of imagination and visualization
- Throat → Inability to express yourself
- Heart → Fear & resistance to change, failure to experience growth
- Solar plexus → Inability to connect outer world with your inner energy
- Sacral → Imbalanced sexual energy
- Root → Feeling disconnected from the world

Dangerous smokers - Individuals belonging to the first category often experience fear when seeking counseling from doctors or psychologists, as this fear is interconnected with their underlying muladhara blockage. They are constantly reminded of their compromised health due to their deep-rooted addiction to smoking, which they perceive as their sole source of joy in life. Consequently, they find themselves trapped in a difficult situation. To escape their fear, they choose to discontinue their sessions with the doctor or psychologist, erroneously believing that this will alleviate their concerns. However, this decision does not address their addiction to smoking, which remains unchanged. As a result, traditional addiction counseling methods may not be effective for individuals in this category.

For such people the only way to quit smoking would be to get rid of that underlying fear. This is the reason why I plan to start CHAKRA ANONYMOUS group (similar to alcohol anonymous) in april 2024. Interested candidates can enroll in the discussion without revealing their true identity to others and can still be part of our life changing chakra discussions. As a moderator I will be allowing each participant to showcase their struggles with their addictions and how they can get to the root cause of their fear first before addressing the smoking addiction.

Underprivileged smokers- second type of smokers, who are involved in activities such as selling drugs, participating in mafia operations, or engaging in criminal behavior due to poverty, often exhibit a lack of concern for the emotional aspects of smoking. They are unlikely to seek help or take quitting seriously, often responding with indifference or amusement when confronted about their smoking habit. Changing the behavior of these individuals can indeed be extremely challenging. However, I agree that education, awareness, and the widespread implementation of practices like yoga and meditation can play a crucial role in preventing the rise of smoking among underprivileged populations. By addressing the underlying causes of their circumstances and providing them with tools for self-reflection and personal growth, we can empower these individuals to make positive changes in their lives before attempting to even quit smoking.

Privileged smokers-third type of smokers can be referred to as privileged smokers. They are individuals who smoke during moments of joy, when facing stressful deadlines, during social gatherings, or after experiencing pleasure. These smokers exhibit rajasic qualities, which are characterized by heightened activity and stimulation, increased partying and socializing activities. Most seem educated and motivated to quit. However, as they mature or grow older, they are more likely to quit smoking and remain non-smokers for life. Only a small percentage of these individuals may eventually become addicted and continue smoking. It is important to acknowledge that the cycle of smoking may persist, albeit to a lesser extent, within this group.

References

- The Yoga sutras of Patanjali by Edwin Bryant.
- Light on yoga by BKS Iyengar.

Made in the USA
Middletown, DE
05 July 2024